WITHDRAWN
UTSA LIBRARIES

DATE DUE

GAYLORD   PRINTED IN U.S.A.

OTHERWISE OCCUPIED

OTHERWISE OCCUPIED

---

*Pedagogies of Alterity and the
Brahminization of Theory*

DOROTHY M. FIGUEIRA

STATE UNIVERSITY OF NEW YORK PRESS

Cover photograph: Duncan Searl, *World Trade Center*, 1974

Published by
STATE UNIVERSITY OF NEW YORK PRESS, ALBANY

For information, contact State University of New York Press, Albany, NY
www.sunypress.edu

Production, Laurie Searl
Marketing, Anne M. Valentine

Library of Congress Cataloging-in-Publication Data

Figueira, Dorothy M.
    Otherwise occupied : pedagogies of alterity and the brahminization of theory / Dorothy M. Figueira.
        p. cm.
    Includes bibliographical references and index.
    ISBN 978-0-7914-7573-7 (hardcover : alk. paper)
    1. Criticism—History—20th century.   2. Postmodernism.
3. Multiculturalism.   I. Title.

PN94.F49 2008
801'.950904—dc22   2008000119

10 9 8 7 6 5 4 3 2 1

CONTENTS

ACKNOWLEDGMENTS

Thirty years of personal experience within academe have gone into the composition of this volume. My career as a literary scholar was marked by my initial formation in France as a student in the social sciences. I began my studies attending the lectures of Lévi-Strauss in Paris and ended in the States as a student of Ricoeur and Gadamer. I came to comparative literature relatively late, after training as an historian of religions. This initial formation, perhaps, made me particularly insouciant regarding the theoretical gods for whom literary scholars were establishing altars in the 80s. Having already studied truly powerful deities, I remember thinking what paltry gods critics were now worshiping. As an Indologist, I witnessed with amazement the movement of India as a site of academic inquiry—from Harappan seals to the English novel. My experience as a first-generation "Hispanic"-American female has afforded me first-hand knowledge of affirmative action protocols and inspired interest in the politics of recent trends in identity studies. As a New Yorker, I was deeply effected, as we all were, by the events of September 11. As a critic, however, I was struck by how the ensuing discourse reflected themes that had become commonplace in the literature classroom. Moreover, all these experiences inform how I conceptualize my work and decode the profession. They also permit me to acknowledge how important it *still* is to have a "face that fits" the establishment. Woe to those who don't!

I want to thank colleagues who have encouraged me and allowed me to present my thoughts in their classrooms and conferences—Jüri Talvet, (Tartu), Monika Schmitz-Emans (Bochum), Sergio Perosa (Venice/NYU), Satish Alekar (Pune), Manfred Schmeling (Saarbrücken), Koji Kawamoto (Tokyo), Chandra Mohan (Delhi), Meng Hua (Beijing), Jean Bessière (Paris), and Jasbhir Jain (Jaipur). I also want to thank colleagues such as Ronald Bogue and Farley Richmond (both of the University of Georgia), Gerald Gillespie (Stanford), John Burt Foster (George Mason University), and Alfred Lopez (Purdue University). I am deeply grateful to Jenny Webb for all her assistance in helping me clean up the manuscript and check sources. I am also indebted to the comments of diligent anonymous readers and the most able editorial staff of the SUNY Press, especially Laurie Searl. I would also like to thank Nancy Ellegate of SUNY Press with whom I have had occasion to work in the past. I much appreciate how the SUNY Press has supported and marketed my work over the years. I would also like to thank my daughters Lila and Mira for their understanding. My husband John has been my ideal reader—insightful and constructive. I dedicate this book to my brothers, Thomas and Robert, who were born too early to benefit from their liminality.

INTRODUCTION

In the last two decades, there has occurred a paradigm shift from the aesthetic to the political. Due to a gradual radicalization of theory, one could reject literature as an outmoded form of cultural capital belonging to the bourgeoisie. By replacing the canon of dead white males with a cultural studies model, critics sought to dismantle the literary canon and install a more immediate and less conservative hierarchical format. In the process, they discovered a novel marketing strategy in the development of a new commodity—the third world. Theories and pedagogies came into being to market radical alterity as a hypercommodity. This book examines how the Other was configured, (mis)represented, (de)formed, and marketed. We chart this construction as it passes from anthropology to the most self-referential forms of literary theory, from cold-war formulations of area studies to the aftermath of September 11.

A general thesis of this volume is that theories and pedagogies of alterity, such as multiculturalism and postcolonialism, inform a larger debate in American academe concerning race. They provide postmodern critiques that shift attention from empirical methodology to the scrutiny of the foundational assumptions of Western rationality and expose how power is imbricated in the material practice of discourses and institutional structures. Our starting point is French structuralism, since Lévi-Strauss introduced themes that have become significant markers in the conceptualization of the Other in the intervening decades. The formulation of the Other in structuralism became crucial to poststructuralist constructions of identity, especially to theoretical discussions regarding the nature of the Self. It is, therefore, important to understand structuralist and poststructuralist concepts of 'history' and 'subjectivity.' Structuralism and poststructuralism also informed subsequent critical theories regarding the role of the critic and the status of the text. Chapter 1 provides a brief overview of the structuralist and poststructuralist precursors to recent critical theories and pedagogies of alterity.

Chapters 2 through 4 analyze the philosophies behind multiculturalism and postcolonialism as well as their institutionalization. Multiculturalism
and postcolonialism arose in an attempt to uncover occluded and submerged
identities in order to liberate the repressed through the dissemination of
peoples' histories. They promote a postmodern vision of the fragmented and
disconnected Self best exemplified by a new type of intellectual, defined as
someone who claims to have dispensed with territorial affiliation and travels
unencumbered through the world bearing the burden of a unique yet representative sensibility. In addition to multicultural and postcolonial subjects,
nomads and exiles also appear in critical discussions. They too refract a hybridized and contingent condition. Chapter 5 explores their arrival on the
theoretical stage. All these figures of migrancy raise questions regarding the
postmodern condition, the role of third-world immigrants, and their function within metropolitan academic institutions. The nomad and the exile, in
particular, embody alterity in its purest form—as metaphors for the Other
who need not even be othered.

The institutionalization of multiculturalism, postcolonialism, and nomadism presents a form of commodity fetishism or the veiling of the material circumstances under which a commodity is produced and consumed.
Commodity fetishism has three components. It involves a mystification or
leveling out of historical experience. It also exhibits an imagined access to
the cultural Other. Finally, it entails the reification of people and places into
aesthetic objects, presenting a historical past more informed by ideology than
by historical and linguistic facts. This distorted vision, dissociated from reality,
is further circumscribed by the critic's strategies of self-representation. Critics
often coopt the position of the Other as paradigms of alterity. The vocabulary
that articulates these conceits appears liberating to many, but not to all. By
bandying about images of flight, literary critics codify notions of universal
and equal mobility that exist only in their theories.

The theories and pedagogies described in these pages conform to the
process that I have termed "brahminization," wherein critics seek to reify their
own position within both their professional and their ethnic communities. In
chapter 4, I argue that the hermeneutic task of the brahmin with regard to
scripture has been assumed by literary critics who appropriate the voice of
the marginalized Other and become professional spokespersons for alterity.
They "brahminize" themselves by claiming the power to disseminate images
of a national culture and its internal Others, documenting and managing the
Other through an objectifying discourse. In the process, they produce what
Bourdieu has termed "cultural capital," a literary field as a site of struggle in
which what is at stake is the power to impose a dominant definition of the

writer and thereby delimit the population entitled to take part in the struggle to define those authorized to call themselves writers. Critics thus assume the task of consecrating both the producers and their products.

Theories of alterity enable critics to establish pedagogies based on the moral presumption of the individual teacher as the self-appointed custodian and transmitter of a text's allegedly oppositional values. Multiculturalism, postcolonialism, and nomadology all structure their belief systems on a nostalgia or yearning for a true cause. Academic spokespersons for the oppressed see themselves as avatars of 1960s activists for social and political justice. The efforts of the alterity pedagogues are grounded in identitarian politics. Their gestures of self-creation betray a comprehensive need that is both utilitarian and emotional: to exercise power and install a history and value system to legitimize themselves and their place in the world. These critical constructions of alterity ultimately contribute to the formation of what can be termed "Occidentalism." Chapter 6 examines how these various theories of alterity came into play in academic and general discourse after the events of September 11.

We can acknowledge that, in certain respects, the Orientalist critique spawned by Edward Said's groundbreaking work in the 1970s rewrote history. It did so, however, only partially. The criticism of Orientalism provided a one-sided apologia regarding Western sins and sinners without addressing the flip side. Examining the East to see if it too might be cluttered with stereotypes or misconceptions was never a sustained part of this critique. Focusing on the past sins of the colonizers and present-day threats from globalism draws attention away from the dehumanizing trends in the East toward itself and its Other, the West. Postcolonial elites, who have internalized Euro-American models and ideals as part of self-fashioning to prepare themselves for power, have not adequately analyzed their relationship to the West. There has been little inquiry into the manner in which theories and pedagogies of alterity serve academic politics. Chapter 7 investigates how these theories and pedagogies have influenced notions of race and the impact they have had upon affirmative action.

The case can be made that identity studies have been used by institutions and individuals to address racial politics within academe. The literary academic pseudohermeneutics examined in these pages hides an ambition for power under a veil of cultural ignorance in the hopes of establishing the domination of a new university elite. The strategies of Hindu brahmins, described by European and Indian authors alike as ritualistic, sometimes unscrupulous, and learned become the central metaphor to describe this process. Just as brahmins jealously and exclusively interpreted the Vedas as foundational texts to serve their dogmatic cause, so too do the critical "brahmins" described in these pages construct reality and contribute to the continued disenfranchisement of minorities. They offer a contemporary strategy that brings together the persistence of romantic and linguistic myths of the nineteenth century, as they have been recuperated by modern theorists, with a racial ideology that resurfaces in academic Occidentalism. Through this brahminization of theory, strategies of power originating in India are adapted and deployed in the world of university criticism. This volume seeks to provide analysis of this process that has been heretofore cruelly lacking in anthropological, literary, and philosophical studies.

CHAPTER 1

CRITICAL BACKGROUND TO POSTSTRUCTURALIST THEORIES AND PEDAGOGIES OF ALTERITY

The Positivist tradition of Auguste Comte valued knowledge that borrowed from a scientific model and transformed itself into a system, understood as an ensemble of scientific changes. Systems (or, as they came to be called, structures) became increasingly important in the development of various academic disciplines. For anthropology, in particular, structure would become a key concept. The principal theorist of what would be called the "structuralist" trend in anthropology was Claude Lévi-Strauss. Before structuralism, ethnography had been linked to the natural sciences, especially the physical anthropology that had dominated the nineteenth century. Lévi-Strauss was innovative in that he sought a new model for anthropology in the social sciences and, especially, in linguistics. The linguistic distinction between synchrony (the signifier) and diachrony (the signified) formulated by Ferdinand de Saussure (1915) came to be interpreted by Lévi-Strauss as the distinction between structure (signifier) and meaning (signified). The alliance that Lévi-Strauss would draw between linguistics and anthropology proved pivotal for literary theory in the latter half of the twentieth century.

Lévi-Strauss also brought to prominence the role of the unconscious, as it is mediated through language. Sigmund Freud had claimed that the unconscious governed society, and Emile Durkheim had acknowledged the unconscious workings of collective practices. Freud and Durkheim would influence structuralism's quest for the hidden mechanisms underlying all textualities. Structural anthropology's examination of the Other would become analogous to psychoanalysis's examination of the estranged Self. Just as psychoanalysis gave access to the Self and sought to represent the Other in the repressed libido and unconscious, ethnology now gave access to the foreign Other revealing the repressed of history.

What was marginal could now be justified and even celebrated philosophically. The sociologist Jean Duvignaud would appoint Lévi-Strauss the vicar of the tropics, pursuing a nostalgic dream of mankind's original purity as had the Savoyard vicar of Jean-Jacques Rousseau (Dosse 1991:1.179).[1] With this quip, Duvignaud touched upon a significant characteristic of Lévi-Strauss's anthropology: its romanticism. Lévi-Strauss had a tendency to relativize behavior on culturalist grounds and trade in nostalgic guilt, traits that would inspire *tiers-mondistes* who had been radicalized by the Algerian War (Lilla 2001:168). However, it was his valorization of the exotic marginalized Other and application of a presumed scientific method that make Lévi-Strauss an important figure for our investigation. It is fitting, therefore, that we begin our study by evoking his work. Structuralism would become a model for those areas of study in the social sciences and humanities that lacked formalism (anthropology, sociology, psychoanalysis, literary criticism) but would themselves become important disciplines in the postwar period.

It should be noted that much of the intellectual ferment engendered by structuralism arose from the waning influence of Sartrean existentialism in the 1960s, especially its notion of a transcendental abstract subject that was singular in its otherness. Structuralism provided an attractive alternative to existentialism. In lieu of the existential subject, it offered the immobility of structures and thus decentered (if not, extinguished) that same subject. It provided an opportunity for those who wanted to distance themselves from Sartre, his "idealism," and the inconsistencies of existentialism.

Structuralism also offered an alternative to phenomenology, whose main proponents in the 1960s were Paul Ricoeur and Emmanuel Levinas. Ricoeur's hermeneutics opposed the structural logic that held to a system of relations made autonomous from content and, subsequently, open to infinite interpretation. Ricoeur did not reject the scientificity of structuralism per se, but he contested what he saw as its transgression of limits. Structuralism was legitimate only so long as it remained conscious of the conditions of its validity (Ricoeur 1963:605). Levinas touted ethics, believing that everything began with the rights of others and our obligation to them. He used phenomenology to distinguish between the Same and the Other and established an ethics based on their copresence (Dosse 1991:2.284). Structuralist anthropology proposed a more radical project. It claimed to address questions regarding the Other by seeking to exhume primitive peoples from the place in which Eurocentrism had interred them.[2]

Structuralism's focus on permanent invariables, synchrony, and hermetic texts essentially questioned the conditions necessary for articulating scientific knowledge. A similar inquiry would be initiated in the sciences by Thomas Kuhn. In *The Structure of Scientific Revolutions* (1962), Kuhn presented science as created from discontinuous, flexible, temporary theories. Science now came to be understood as a creation of perspectives. One could reject the objectivity of knowledge in favor of "discourses."[3] Once objective truth was called into question, the writing of history soon followed suit. Thanks to structuralism's disavowal of historical context, search for origins, diachrony, and teleology, history now became a text open to various disparate interpretations. In *Écrits* (1966), Jacques Lacan rejected the notion that history had any meaning, claiming it to be an illusion. Only analytic discourse could give voice to the unconscious and historical. The present could be seen as an eternal recycling of different configurations of the past. In this process, the traditional subject was split, reduced, and dethroned.

Two Bulgarian emigrés, who perhaps carried the burden of history more than their native-born French colleagues, recognized the limitations of the structuralist model. In order to acknowledge the historical fabric in which a text was written, Julia Kristeva resuscitated the element of subjectivity, not, however, the classical subject, but the fragmented Self described by Lacan. Kristeva's compatriot, Tzevan Todorov, shared her *méfiance* with certain aspects of structuralism. Todorov, who knew firsthand totalitarian reality, saw a form of Stalinistic dogmatism in the obligatory reading grids that structural criticism imposed. This concern was shared by the sociologist Pierre Bourdieu who questioned the hegemonic role of institutional positions. Bourdieu studied how social actors, even those who considered themselves free from social determinism, were influenced by outside forces. Like Kristeva, Bourdieu also wanted to reintroduce agents that had been lost as epiphenomena of structure. By installing the subjectivity of the non–Cartesian subject, Bourdieu sought not the ego, but the individual trace of an entire collective history (Bourdieu 1987:40). However, fearing a new legitimization of philosophical discourse and a corporatist defense of privilege that allowed intellectuals to continue to judge the criteria of scientificity, Bourdieu specifically warned against theories that allow theorists to act as guardians before the temple, denounce deviation, and form a priesthood.

There was indeed a clear paradox inherent in structuralist theory. While intellectuals were ostensively working for change and developing theoretical weapons to advance a progressive struggle, they were at the same time be-ing seduced by a paradigm that stifled all desire for change and announced the end of history (Dosse 1991:2.72). With a vengeance, May 1968 would exhume history and the subject that structuralism had repressed. The *Annales* historians, in particular, were beneficiaries of 1968, since they were able to transform "History" into "histories" (Veyne 1971). History was still discovering the Other. However, this Other was not in other lands, but could now be studied within Western civilization in the form of cultural histories and the study of *mentalités*.[4] Anthropology's Other had become its own past and values. Sometimes the Other became just the theorist's present. Simone de Beauvoir's mandarins of existentialism became Kristeva's samurai in the new cult of personality.[5] Criticism turned its attention to the discovery of the Self and its pleasures, in the case of Barthes,[6] or in the case of Kristeva, its abjection. While it may seem to be truly the grand return of the repressed subject, it would be a mistake to think that the Self had not always been present for theorists.

It became increasingly fashionable to situate onself at the edges of a system of thought in order to manipulate and move those edges. We were no longer interested in the hell of others, but the hell in the Self. In the *Archaeology of Knowledge,* Michel Foucault claimed that man was an invention of recent date soon to disappear (Foucault 1972:387). He championed the destruction of history, faceless writing, and pure freedom (Foucault 1972:17). The idea was to decenter man as author, subject, and speaker. Georges Canguilhem's work on psychology (asking whether it served science or the police) set the stage for Foucault's work on asylums, prisons, and madness. Self-awareness regarding the limits of knowing others now became a precondition for engagement. Foucault focused on the periphery and the margins of a system. He analyzed the development of European civilization as a process of marginalizing domestic misfits who were kept under surveillance through the cooperation of social "power" and "knowledge." He further examined deviation and marginality in *Discipline and Punish* (1975). *The History of Sexuality* (1976) offered a discourse on sex as a form of managerial power found in censuses and the psychiatrization of deviation. The structuralist ideal had shifted from a scientific method informed by political and cultural pessimism into a liberation antitheology celebrating difference, wherever it might be found.

The *Gulag Archipelago* had appeared in 1974. With it, Solzhenitsyn brought the 1956–67 reality of totalitarianism to the attention of Western scholars who could now no longer blithely choose to ignore its real dimensions. In the wake of Solzhenitsyn, critical theories that had evolved from an impassioned critique of democracy and its institutions ideally should have undergone reevaluation. To a significant degree, they did not. Louis Althusser, for example, continued to theorize socialism without confronting its reality.

He was not forced to reflect on the historical lessons drawn from the disaster of the Soviet Union. Academic Marxism's essentialisms did not allow logical consequences to be drawn from the totalitarian reality, even after the events in Czechoslovakia of August 1968 and Cambodia in 1977.

The Gulag showed that all you had to do was look, listen, and read. It posed a real problem for structuralist Marxism: why, in its quest for hidden logic, did it even now refuse to grant validity to empirical reality? From an objective point of view, structuralism could even be viewed as complicit with the torturers, when, after having eliminated subjectivity in order to gain access to science, it deconstructed the dissidents' message of human rights violations (Dosse 1991:2.271).[7] Now it was not clear if one could even appeal to reason in forming judgment, since language and social structure loomed so large. The term *man* began to appear in quotations marks; man was now a site, a point where various social, cultural, economic, linguistic, and psychological forces intersected. This radical antihumanism ushered in the age of deconstruction.

Deconstruction arose in response to the scientific aspirations of speculative structuralism, whose methods and categories had derived from linguistics. Derrida viewed language as a form of death and called for the radical decentering of the implicit hierarchies imbedded in language that had encouraged us to do things such as place speech above writing, author above reader, and signified above signifier. Deconstruction's task was to reveal the aporiae and paradoxes imbedded in every text. Since all texts contain ambiguities, they can be read in different ways (*la différence*) with exhaustive interpretation forever deferred (*la différance*). The end of logocentrism, the naive notion that language was a transparent medium, would bring about the end of all bad centrisms, such as (to cite Derrida himself) andro-, phalo-, phallologo- or carnophallologocentrism. Derrida's project, however, led to an obvious problem. If language cannot make unambiguous claims, how can one use language to make deconstruction's claims (Lilla 2001:172–73)? This unbreachable paradox at the heart of deconstruction was brought into full relief in the de Man disclosures of 1987,[8] when the politics that deconstruction had playfully left suspended had to be addressed.

In the *Politiques de l'amitié* (1988–89 seminar), Derrida made an initial response: the entire Western tradition of thinking about politics was distorted by philosophy's original sin—the concept of "identity." All natural categories and their derivative concepts of "community," "culture," and "nation" are dependent on language and, therefore, conventions that establish hierarchies. If political philosophy had no center, and the methods of political philosophy were suspected of logocentrism, there was not much to be done. All political ideologies were equally unacceptable because they were logocentrist. There are no tyrants, wicked institutions, gulags, or genocides, just the tyranny of language that causes tyranny (Lilla 2001:178). Thus, it becomes futile to advocate human rights or condemn crimes against humanity. Derridean deconstruction made it difficult to distingiush between right and wrong: all such notions are infected with logocentrism.

Barbara Johnson recognized deconstruction's disregard for social injustice and general indifference to gender and ethnicity. On the eve of the de Man scandal, she published *The World of Difference* (1987), challenging text-based theory (*différance*) and advocating the social studies approach of identitarianism. The rise of American academic feminism and its valorization of the study of race, ethnicity, and gender provided a further response to the perception that agency had become irrelevant to theory. The late 1980s witnessed the emergence of African American, Latino, Native American, and Asian American studies, to be followed by postcolonial and cultural studies. The appearance of these fields announced that the age of deconstructive close readings was over. Beyond logocentrism, there was indeed agency and identity. The rhetoric of agency (Rajan 2002:37) that had been lost through Derridean deconstruction was now being reintroduced into theory.

Critics such as Fredric Jameson blamed politically counterproductive tendencies in structuralism and poststructuralism for the absence of agency. Structuralism and Marxism had clearly failed to deliver sufficiently revolutionary agents for social change. Theory now sought alternatives to the bourgeois formulation of the individual. Minorities became ideal candidates as new revolutionary agents who could live in conflict with their subject positions. We begin to find in theory, therefore, a valorization and privileging of those whose lives articulate social contradictions, people whose particular situation as subjects in society was seen as atypical or conflicted. Often these "minorities" were minority only in the loosest sense of the term. Few Puerto Ricans from the barrio or inner-city blacks were publishing discourses on their subject positions. The minorities in question were often culled from elite third-world zones. They understood the proper stance to assume as individuals of color within predominantly white academe. Figures such as Said and Gayatri Spivak appeared on the scene as emissaries of this newly valorized revolutionary hyphenated subjectivity. Significantly, revolutionary subjectivities could also be constituted in terms of sexuality and body politics. The salient point to note in the construction of such subjectivities is that the individuals themselves can construct and even alter them at will. The ability to self-identify subjectivity would become an increasingly attractive option.

Ernesto Laclau and Chantal Mouffe contributed significantly to this debate. They represented the subject as an always incomplete articulation to be deformed at any time (Laclau and Mouffe 1985:111). In a subsequent non-co-authored piece, "Hegemony and the New Political Subject," Mouffe presents a more imaginary understanding of the subject as comprising multiple possible constructions (Nelson and Grossberg 1988:90). The subject position here becomes the equivalent of social position and social relations based on received ideas of social identity such as gender, religion, nationality, and race. The subject could now be understood in terms of its social role and construction of self-identity.

The concept of "self-fashioning" also found expression in the work of Rosalind Coward and John Ellis. In *Language and Materialism: Developments in Semiology and the Theory of the Subject* (1977), they conceived the subject in terms of identity construction as opposed to any deconstruction into psychological, linguistic, or social registers. In their schema, the concept of the Other becomes crucial to social analysis. This self-fashioning involved not just willed action but also social behavior of individuals who belong to groups (men, women, immigrants, ethnic minorities) in order to situate human activities within a polemic of values and strategies (beliefs, projects, political interests). This vision of self-fashioning reappeared in the movements that would come into prominence—new historicism, cultural studies, and, as we shall see, the theories and pedagogies of alterity to be examined in this volume. New historicism drew inspiration from Foucault in its attempt to bring back agency. Its concept of the Self, as articulated by Stephen Greenblatt, was alternately both representative and performative, self-fashioned and culturally fashioned. Such a notion of the precarious and provisionally fixed subject was also pivotal to cultural studies.

In structuralism, actions were only socially significant when given meaning by a symbolic structure that was always already in place. For decades, critics had believed that meaning was semiotically mediated through symbolic forms, kinship structures, archetypes, rhetorical tropes, bureaucratic practices, and cultural texts. Language and literature scholars were now beginning to give themselves completely over to the contrary paradigm. In their formulation of cultural studies, Grossberg, Nelson, and Treichler (1992) posited the primacy of social acts. Their paradigm was different from earlier paradigms of cultural studies as found in Barthes's *Mythologies* (1957) or Baudrillard's *Le système des objets* (1968) with their emphases on taxonomies of semiotics, linguistics, and rhetorical shifts from representation to performance. The battle lines had changed. Instead of the orthodox Marxist invoking class struggle as the best means to transform society, the new cultural studies critics recognize other identitarian social formations with revolutionary potential such as race, sexual orientation, and ethnicity (Rapaport 2001:104). The identity paradigm adopted by the poststructuralist and postdeconstructive theories examined in the following pages holds the social subject accountable for the social expression not as mere representations, but as social acts having direct consequences on the lives of others.[9] The important message of the social act paradigm is that a connection must always be made to token representation. In addition to being representative, it is also important to be singular.

Jean-Luc Nancy in *La communauté désoeuvrée* (1986) theorized on the singularity of being as not generalizable, universalizable, or unifiable. Nancy's thesis utilized Heidegger's understanding of the inappropriability of being. Drucilla Cornell then applied this notion of being to women and minorities who become seen in terms of their singularity as Others (Rapaport 2001:143). Cornell's subject is marked not only as Other but also as an Other with a preestablished social identity (Jew, Gay, Latino, female). This intentional and performative vision of subjectivity can also be found in the gender analysis of Judith Butler. For these theorists, as for Foucault, the position of the social subject is both self- and culturally fashioned. Most important, it is always encountered in conflict.

In the 1990s, American academe learned to read the subject in a role of opposition and, as such, in terms of its marginality. Literature, in turn, came to be seen as a social text serving the purposes of activism. As a consequence to the political turn in theory, interpretation became less complicated for its practitioners than it had been under deconstruction. Readers now needed only to extract those social facts necessary to attain the desired politically effective agenda. The singularity of the subject, however, demanded a close identification with subalternity and this identification posed the threat of appropriation. As Peggy Kamuf noted, the politics of academe often involves a struggle for the appropriation of the Other and an attempt to coopt the singularity of subjecthood (Kamuf 1997:121). Never has this problem been more prevalent than in recent literary theory.

In the succeeding pages, we will investigate instances where a politics of appropriation informs theory and pedagogy. We will question what has been the objective of truth seeking in the various critical schools that have developed. We will also ask who benefits and who loses in such endeavors. In whose interests have notions of agency been gained or lost? Who speaks for whom and toward what purpose? We will investigate how the "isms" that succeeded structuralism examine the relationship between culture and power, representation and social equality (Chow 2002:113). Literature has become a social document or social text for the purpose of political activism within the university (Rapaport 2001:93). It serves as a vehicle for forms of social contestation (Donaghue 1987). In other words, theory has become the best of all possible spiritual and material worlds (Chow 2002:106–07). Rather than being perceived as inhabiting an ivory tower where theorists merely study theory, academics can see and present themselves as manning the barricades. They become part of a process of changing the world for the better (Rapaport 2001:93). In fact, they assume roles similar to that of the public intellectuals of the 1930s, epitomized by Sartre. They can embody the same paradox of positionality that Camus recognized in Sartrean existentialism—its emphasis on political engagement (Judt 1998:91). It is not only the contradictions of the public intellectual and the modern critic that are similar, but also the ensuing reification of the Self, what Raymond Aron was to call their posture as "*agrégés-théologiens*" or, to cite Camus, "*juges-penitents*" (cited in Judt 1998:180). Inconsistencies of positionality and hybris formed the legacy that Sartre bequeathed to the next generation of French thinkers. It would have a brilliant career with them and be exported abroad.

CHAPTER 2

MULTICULTURALISM

Is our lack of knowledge of languages and cultures of the Muslim world a sign that multiculturalism has failed?

—*New York Times* Poll, November 2001

SIMULATED BATTLES

For Southerners, the last American war was the Civil War. There are few monuments to or evocations of the First and Second World Wars and almost no mention of Korea. Veneration of Vietnam veterans is real but pales next to the monumental presence of the Civil War. This disregard for subsequent engagements does not stem from the fact that the South did not supply the majority of the white Americans who fought these wars. Rather, it is because the Civil War eclipses all other wars and remains a fresh wound in the Southern psyche.[1] For this reason, one finds in the South the curious ritual known as the Civil War Reenactment. Men, often fathers and sons, get together on weekends to reenact battles. Dressed in authentic period uniforms, with authentic arms, they converge at dawn upon historic Civil War sites. My informants have explained to me that the reenacts are primarily a hobby for history buffs. They claim that by staging reenactments they fight historical ignorance. There is the belief that people have "twisted and retold Southern history into something it's not. . . . We reenact these battles to show the mostly misinformed public what the war was really like and what it was really about."[2]

In the following chapters, I wish to take this ritual as a framing argument to discuss a phenomenon that I have witnessed within American academe. I will investigate how a politics of resentment functions paradigmatically to

define critical and pedagogical gestures of inclusion within American universities. In particular, I will examine how the institutionalization of identity
studies within academe, in the form of multiculturalism and postcolonialism,
provide two terms of a rhetorical syllogism informing a larger debate concerning mandated curricular diversity. It is my thesis that theories and pedagogies of alterity have been constructed as responses to affirmative action. In
this chapter, I will investigate how multiculturalism serves a similar symbolic
purpose on the university level that the Civil War reenactment plays on the
social level.[3] The conflict in this instance is not the Civil War, but the civil
rights battle. In both cases, "the noble war" becomes the metaphor for communities wishing to assert a political identity that is at odds with reality. Just
as the white Southerner rewrites history in his reenactment, so too does the
academic. Both seek self-validation through the gestural. Both identify with
victims of repression on a level of representation.

THE INSTITUTIONALIZATION
OF MULTICULTURALISM

Nine years ago, after years of working in the Northeast and Midwest, I
assumed the headship of a comparative literature department at the University
of Georgia. My department holds fifteen full lines and a curriculum that, in
addition to teaching regular courses in comparative literature and theory, teaches
language and literature courses in Chinese, Japanese, Korean, Zulu, Yoruba,
Swahili, Vietnamese, and Hindi. Comparative literature at the University of
Georgia is a department that truly has the potential to deal with the globe
more responsibly than most comparative literature departments. However, a
curious situation arose that rendered this department and the teaching of
world literature useless to the undergraduate population.

In Georgia, we have what a colleague of mine has termed the "meeting of two incommensurables." There was a university mandate demanding
courses in cultural diversity. This mandate could either be read in a narrow
sense (domestic diversity) or broadly (as globalism). On the university level,
those wanting the narrow focus lost the debate. On the college level, however,
cultural diversity was understood as multiculturalism, and multiculturalism was
defined as domestic. The level of the discussion was not particularly sophisticated.
Those who favored an international focus were accused of being Eurocentric
racists or working a racially motivated flank maneuver. Given the state's racist
history (blacks were not admitted to the University until 1961 and almost
immediately required state trooper protection), this rhetoric was effective. The
practical effects on the college level are as follows. To meet the multicultural
requirement, most of the course material must consist of American ethnic

literature (African American, Latino American, Korean American literatures). While any number of English literature courses can fulfill the undergraduate literature core and multicultural requirements, world literature by definition cannot. Sections of world literature classes, now empty, are dropped from the curriculum in favor of domestic multicultural courses. The heritage of the world's literature is rendered less valuable than the output of two hundred years of American literary production.

Another curious situation arose. In the institutionalization of multiculturalism, an American ethnic experience such as black American culture becomes "othered": it was rendered foreign, no matter how inextricably bound it is to American culture. The study of literature has assumed a rather limited and didactic function. One reads in order to learn social tolerance. What used to be the job of parents or organized religion has now fallen to the university. The administration pretends that their students have more of a chance of learning to live in harmony if they read Maya Angelou rather than Wole Soyinka. In this instance, an institution with little real diversity mimes cultural diversity, "a genteel phrase for ethnic and racial parity and sometimes for affirmative action" (Jacoby 1994b:123). What began as an attempt to combat the existence and/or perception of endemic racism resulted in defining globalism within the narrow focus of the American ethnic experience. The motive might have been sincere, albeit naive. In its institutionalization, it became exclusionary and provincial.

But there was a more pressing agenda at work. The state of Georgia is 29.8 percent black (2000 Census). In Spring 2008, according to its Office of Instructional Research, only 6 percent of the undergraduate population in the largest state university are black. Rather than address the problems posed by the institutional climate, the answer is to put "minority" courses on the books and impel the nonminority students to elect them. The logic here is significant. Classes presumably dealing with alterity absolve institutions for not confronting real problems of diversity. Showcase racial tolerance can thus be imposed on a nonminority population. Students recognize the politics of such university gestures and are vocal and insouciant in their resentment. Moreover, and perhaps more disturbing, administrators believe that minorities can be "bought," if given what they supposedly want—courses on their historic victimization or reaffirming their identity as Other within the American continuum.

While department head, I raised the issue of domestic multiculturalism as the institutionalized "monopoly of suffering." Along with several colleagues, I petitioned the University Senate to broaden the multicultural requirement to include source cultures, that is, teach African American literature in the context of the African literary models that informed black American voices. There was a spectacular confrontation within the Senate. In our camp, Asianists, Africanists,

Europeanists were suggesting that courses in African American literature might best be taught if contextualized within the African framework, showing how literary forms derive from their source culture. The other camp had invited to the debate all the black faculty (a handful) and emailed the black operational staff (hundreds) to accuse us of Eurocentric racism. These black faculty and staff accepted the script that a "department of Europeanists" was trying to remove their heritage from the curriculum. This was never the case; we were, rather, trying to teach it in a more comprehensive manner. I was operating on the premise, articulated by Henry Louis Gates in *The Signifying Monkey* (1988) that the history of a people is reckoned through the internal logic of their own culture, and we must understand that logic in order to understand their achievement. I felt that this should be the task of multiculturalism.

But, perhaps, the more telling discourse was that of the white academics and administrators. Their argument was that courses in domestic multicultural- ism were synonymous with the civil rights battles of the 1960s. They evoked solidarity with the Reverend Martin Luther King Jr. There were even teary- eyed testimonials by white middle-aged professors claiming that their efforts in the University Senate were akin to marching with Dr. King. Let us place this discourse into context. Almost all of these white professors were too young to have been involved with civil rights action in the South. Their militancy consisted in most cases of avoiding the Vietnam draft. Nevertheless, they felt they had the right to invoke this "true" struggle and to place themselves by proxy in the camp of the virtuous. Critical rhetoric had afforded them the luxury to coopt the suffering of the Other and claim it as their own, even if their master narrative was the consolidation of power within their paltry university departments.

Listening to the senate debate that I had initiated, I found myself drawing an alternate analogy between these professors and Southern Civil War reenac- tors. Like the hobbyist Southerners who spend their weekends reenacting the Civil War battles, it seemed that these academics were reenacting civil rights battles. Both sought compensation for their liminality from actual struggle in a posture of militancy by proxy. The Southern heritage enthusiast at least exercises at dawn with his son; the academic wages a sordid departmental political battle for additional funding allocation, office space, and sabbatical leave. The institutionalization of multiculturalism provided the battle flag around which these academic-robed troops could convene.

THE METHODOLOGY OF MULTICULTURALISM

In *Mapping Multiculturalism*, Avery F. Gordon and Christopher Newfield have also made a connection between multiculturalism and civil rights protocols.[4]

They questioned if multiculturalism was, indeed, a characteristic product of the post–civil rights period and whether it had aided or hindered civil rights (Gordon and Newfield 1996:10). They traced it back to the efforts in the 1970s to reorganize education for the benefit of minority students and dismantle white majority control of schools and the use of white values as the sole yardstick of excellence. Multiculturalism, according to these theorists, was an attempt to recover lost knowledge and produce a new understanding of U.S. history.

The institutionalization of multiculturalism in the United States is not only a bureaucratic structure purporting to foster minority rights. It can also be seen as an outgrowth of the movement in the 1980s on American campuses to revamp the canon. Multiculturalism claims to open the canon up to subalterns, exiles, and others. Ideally, it should facilitate dead white males being supplanted by authors from underrepresented groups in curricula and dead-wood white male professors being supplanted by women and minorities. However, its call to reenvision the world from a decolonizing and antiracist perspective has triggered reactions on both the Right and the Left. On the Right, multiculturalism was seen as an attack on Euro-American culture. On the Left, it represented an assault not on Euro-Americans but on Eurocentrism, the discourse that "embeds, takes for granted and normalizes . . . the hierarchical power relations generated by colonialism and imperialism" (Shohat and Stam 2003:7). One of multiculturalism's underlying assumptions is that people comprehend people like themselves, rather than translate difference (Gitlin 1995:208–09). A Stanford University student, when asked during that university's debates over canon revision about studying important non-Western trends such as Japanese capitalism or Islamic fundamentalism, responded: "Who gives a damn about those things? I want to study myself" (San Juan 1995:230–31). The sad truth is that some students of multiculturalism, although they saw themselves as border-crossers or cultural workers (Giroux 1992:21, 23), defined alterity in very self-referential terms, a trait, as we shall see, not unique to their conceptualization of alterity.

Multiculturalism presupposes two basic ideas. First, it recognizes that American history is not solely reflected in the activities of one race (white), one language group (English), one ethnicity (Anglo-Saxon), or one religion (Christianity). It quite correctly claims that African Americans, Latinos, Asian Americans, Native Americans, and others have made central contributions to American culture. It also suggests that beneath the differences among Americans are some underlying principles and values that bring us together. This theory of diversity presupposes and requires the notion of an assimilationist "common culture" and fosters a social order founded on the principle of unity in multiplicity (San Juan 1995:223). It revisions the image of America as a melting pot into America as a salad that is now not only colorful and beautiful but also capable of being consumed. This transformation begs the question: "Who is the consumer?" (Davis 1996:45).

Multiculturalism is not just an epistemological phenomenon. The consumption of multiculturalism within the university replicates that of corporate-level structures, since universities are also corporations (Lubiano 1996:70). We can, therefore, compare multicultural educational practices to corporate diversity management initiatives that assume that racially and ethnically diverse groups need to be managed and controlled in ways to contain conflict and fortify power relations.[5] The corporate model—that is, disciplining diversity as a strategy for more control of workers (Davis 1996:41)—does not attempt to assimilate diversity into the dominant culture. Rather, it digests unassimilated diversity with the same results as if homogeneity prevailed. The control problem with this model is that the cultures of multiculturalism are not the same and cannot be so easily consumed by the dominant white culture. As we shall see, multiculturalism conveniently provides a solution to this problem too.

As the Georgia episode highlights, multiculturalism seeks to include representatives of traditionally neglected groups and offer an alibi for liberal reform that may not, in fact, exist. In this effort, the educational system has manifestly entered the important promotional work of encouraging tolerance, pluralism, and diversity as rearguard damage control (Cruz 1996:32). Under this format, multiculturalism serves as an institution's strategic response to a perceived deterioration of the progressive policies, civil rights gains, and change in demographics.[6] Toward the same goal of teaching tolerance, institutional offices of diversity, workshops at teachers' conventions, publisher's marketing sessions, and curricula in primary and secondary schools throughout America now all target "cultural diversity" and multicultural literacy as prime directives.

Multiculturalism has also been presented as an alternative to the civilizational model made popular by Samuel Huntington in *The Clash of Civilizations and Remaking the World Order* (1996) and others.[7] The civilizational model broadly claims that in the post–Cold War world, conflicts will not be waged between nation-states or along ideological lines, such as capitalism opposing socialism. Rather, conflict will be based on what Huntington terms "civilizational" grounds.[8] It is Huntington's thesis that the West is losing ground and that non-Western civilizations are expanding economically, militarily, and politically by exploiting Western modernization as well as their own indigenous traditions. The non-West culls what the West can offer in terms of technology while at the same time reaffirming the values inherent in and traditional to their own cultures (Huntington 1996:20). According to Huntington, this recognition on the part of non-Western cultures of their inherent strengths has brought about a process of reindigenization, as seen in Hindu and Islamic religious and cultural resurgence. Huntington claims that it is just this type of revival that is needed in the West to bring about a similar resurgence of its civilization. Such a revival is impeded, however, by movements such as multiculturalism that encourage immigrants from other civilizations to reject assimilation and continue to adhere to and propagate the values, customs, and culture of their home societies. Huntington views the multicultural trend as producing a form of schizophrenia that makes America a torn culture (Huntington 1996:304–06). In terms quite similar to the dire prognostications of Gobineau in the nineteenth century, Huntington fears that Western values have so consistently eroded that the West cannot recoup. We are in a process of such internal decay of our values that we cannot respond to external threats upon those same values (Huntington 1996:303). Huntington's Tocquevillian model is simplistic and flawed in many respects, first and foremost being his essentialist understanding of "civilization" as a neutral rubric for a discussion primarily about religion.[9] A refutation of Huntington's civilizational model, however, is not within the purview of this present study. What I would like to highlight, rather, is how Huntington's civilizational model, an inclusive idea that there exists a set of cultural values, is presented as the antithesis of the equally inclusionary institutionalized practice of multiculturalism.

Proponents of multiculturalism portray it as an antidote to the vision of world order offered by Huntington. David Palumbo-Liu views the "clash of civilizations" rhetoric as both a strategy to delegitimize multiculturalism[10] and an attempt to demonize ethnic Americans (Palumbo-Liu 2002:121–22).[11] In Palumbo-Liu's estimation, multiculturalism must be promoted as an agenda of "progressive humanism" (Palumbo-Liu 2002:126–27). He characterized it as the contestatory movement par excellence: an offshoot of 1970s activism, third-world consciousness, antiwar politics, the rise of the New Left, and the burgeoning feminist, gay, and lesbian movements (Palumbo-Liu 2002:116–17). It should not be denigrated; its inherent virtue resides in its claim to promote political inclusion. Multiculturalism should, in fact, be championed as a form of cultural affirmative action (O'Brian and Little 1990).

Stanley Fish does not see multiculturalism as a conscious strategy devised by insurgent political groups desirous of capturing American cultural space. He sees it as unplanned (Fish 1997:388). Fish has identified two forms of multiculturalism operating in American academe today: what he has termed the boutique as opposed to the strong version. Boutique multiculturalism establishes a superficial relationship, wherein students are encouraged to admire and recognize the legitimacy of traditions other than their own. They stop short of approving other cultures when some value at their core generates an act that offends the canons of civilized decency as they have been either declared or assumed. In other words, boutique multiculturalism embraces difference up to the point precisely when it matters most to committed members (Fish 1997:378–79). Strong multiculturalism, in contrast, claims to accord a deep respect to all cultures at their core. Each has the right to form its own identity and nourish its own sense of what is rational and humane (Fish 1997:389). For strong multiculturalists, the first principle is tolerance. Strong multiculturalism works to the point where a culture whose core values you are tolerating reveals itself to be intolerant. At this juncture, you can either stretch your toleration to expand to their intolerance or condemn their core intolerance and therefore no longer accord them respect. The strong multiculturalist usually opts for the latter choice in the name of the suprauniversal. In short, strong multiculturalism reveals itself to be not very strong after all. Essentially, it is not very distinct from boutique multiculturalism, just a deeper instance of what boutique multiculturalism presents in a shallow form (Fish 1997:383).

Fish's article was a response to a debate on the philosophy and ethics of multiculturalism initiated by Charles Taylor (Taylor 1992). Taylor defined multiculturalism as a politics of difference, where the preferred value that is protected and fostered is the unique distinctiveness of the particular (Taylor 1992:43).[12] Multiculturalism is, essentially, the pedagogical praxis of the politics of recognition. In opposition to Taylor's thesis, Steven C. Rockefeller posited our identity within the universal as primary and more fundamental than any particular identity such as citizenship, gender, race, or ethnicity (Rockefeller 1992:88). The universal will win out over the individual because the individual is the foundation of recognition of equal value and the related idea of equal rights. Individual choice cannot be pursued to the point where it interferes with, prescribes, or proscribes the choices of others. Rockefeller's concept promotes a politics of equal dignity in which the local is subordinated to a universal value of free rational choice. Under a politics of equal dignity, shared potential is protected by law and particular forms of its realization (tradition, religion, ethnic allegiances) succeed or fail in the marketplace "give and take" (Fish 1997:381). Fish labeled Taylor's politics of difference as nothing but strong multiculturalism (Fish 1997:382) and Rockefeller's recognition of equal dignity as a form of boutique multiculturalism.

Neither boutique nor strong multiculturalism comes to terms with difference (Fish 1997:385), although their inabilities are asymmetrical. Boutique multiculturalism views the core values of cultures as overlays on a substratum of essential humanity and thus tolerates them without taking them seriously and seeing them as truly core (Fish 1997:379). We are all essentially alike. Boutique multiculturalism views difference in terms of matters of lifestyle. It honors diversity in its most superficial aspects, with a deeper loyalty given to some notion of its universal potential. Strong multiculturalism takes difference seriously as a general principle but cannot take seriously any particular difference that refuses to be generous in its own turn; it cannot allow their imperatives full realization in political programs since it would inevitably lead to the suppression of difference (Fish 1997:386). In these competing notions of recognition, Fish questions where respect for the Other actually resides, in tolerating difference (and, thereby, "disrespecting" it) or in taking it seriously enough to oppose it (Fish 1997:388).[13] He concludes that multiculturalism is ultimately an incoherent concept (Fish 1997:388).

Other critics are equally dismissive in their assessments of multiculturalism's role within university politics. Slavoj Žižek characterized it as an experience of the Other deprived of its Otherness.[14] Wahneema Lubiano condemned multiculturalism as an empty abstraction used by administrators to take the political heat off institutions for their failure to diversify (Lubiano 1996:68). Multiculturalism flourishes as a program while it weakens as a reality (Jacoby 1994b:124), since students are still held to Euro-American values for education and life success (Guerrero 1996:61). Studying the Other in multiculturalism's thoroughly appropriated and diluted fashion ensures that the continued domination of Eurocentric knowledge remains unchallenged. Multiculturalism is then nothing more than a subterfuge for business as usual. One can bring American Indian studies, for example, onto campuses as a "polite pseudo-intellectual vehicle to provide the appearance of ethnic diversity." However, Native American cultural production is not presented as offering an alternative to Eurocentrism and its institutions. It ends up only providing validation to supposed insights and conclusions of Euro-American academia (Guerrero 1996:56).

The key concern here is that identity is not simply a matter of positionality, nor is the multicultural ideology a way to recuperate sensibilities disintegrated by society and the labor market (San Juan 1992:4). Such problems cannot be solved by university canon reform. The neutral shibboleths of difference and diversity cannot replace real-life suffering and struggle for survival and dignity (San Juan 1992:138). The real concern is not just the texts that transmit the heritage of the humanities in order to preserve standards and promote excellence. Rather, we should ask who defines the standards of excellence and whose interests are at stake? Who should articulate the purpose and meaning of a humanities education and how? In other words, who makes the tasty salad, who is meant to consume it, and what is its nutritional value? The multicultural battles at Stanford University over the revision of the canon met with considerable resistance from factions decrying the replacement of the classics from the Western tradition with lesser-valued works from minority literatures. However, part of the resistance also stemmed from what was seen as the cooptative strategy behind such canon revision. Does not the process of liberalizing the canon by simple addition of non-Western texts betoken tokenization (Pratt 1994:59)? If nonwhite materials are perceived as "add-ons" to white structures, they never address the centrality and dominance of the latter or institutional and structural determinants of inequality (Newfield and Gordon 1996:79, 87). Multiculturalism should question old definitions of knowledge and disciplines as defined by a Western canon of texts. Ultimately, difference should make a difference (Davis 1996:48).

The simple fact is that not only conservative think tanks and champions of the Western canon criticized the institutionalization of multiculturalism. Minority critics and students have made their voices heard. At the University of Texas, Chicano students expressed their uneasiness regarding multicultural-ism. They viewed it as a bland, catch-all phrase connected with diversified reading lists or required courses on non-Western cultures. They perceived it as a means of thwarting a head-on confrontation that should take place over institutional racism (San Juan 1995:224). Their perception had a good deal of validity. As an imposition of some norm of tolerance, multiculturalism is inherently a form of control (Essed 1991:210). Satisfied with bracketing the Other, multiculturalism glosses over pressing problems of a political, legal, and economic nature.

In reality, multiculturalism only offers the illusion of victory over racism. It does not dignify anyone, as some have charged, because it does not address the issue of who has the power to determine what courses are taught and what requirements are established (San Juan 1995:224–25). It does, however, beg the question: who really benefits from the identity industry? This is a general question to which we will return in subsequent chapters. At this juncture, one can safely claim that, contrary to its inflated aspirations, multi-culturalism does not guarantee equality of opportunity or access to resources for the disenfranchised. Multiculturalism does not liberate anyone. In fact, the case can be made that it provides a smokescreen for societal and institutional unwillingness to change the academic situation of minorities.

MARKETING THE MARGIN

Even though multiculturalism is more interested in managing the Other within the American continuum than analyzing non-Western reality, the third world is studied in many American universities under the umbrella of multiculturalism. The practical reason for this packaging of alterity is obvious: multiculturalism is easy (Talbot 2001). It does not involve learning about another culture or demand learning another language. As one critic has noted, in multiculturalism each immigrant group preserves its own heritage as long as it speaks English (Prashad 2000:112). Multiculturalism also feeds American isolationism. In the Internet age, when the globalization of English has contributed to diminishing the need to learn other languages, the Other can, thanks to multiculturalism, be consumed "on the cheap." Multiculturalism's celebration of diversity in no way compromises American tendencies to cultural provincialism, triumphalism, or indifference to the world. Like those popular ethnic fairs one finds in the States, multiculturalism allows students to taste other cultures without digesting them.[15] The resounding global education that multiculturalism offers a literature student can consist of nothing more that snippets from Arundhati Roy, Toni Morrison, or Maxine Hong Kingston. Multiculturalism presumes that one can grasp the world by reading selections from representative women of color writing in the English language (Talbot 2001).

Within multiculturalism, there is a real incentive not to respect the intellectual history or genealogy of an area of study. As the domestic multiculturalists at Georgia proved, there is little desire to contextualize the ethnic experience or broaden its significance by drawing any association to a source culture that might extend knowledge beyond the master narrative of multiculturalism. Ann du Cille draws similar conclusions regarding the newfound interest that multiculturalist studies has exhibited for African American women (du Cille 1997:32; cited in Rapaport 2001:2). Multiculturalism appears to honor the field of black feminist studies, but it actually demeans the work by ignoring the fact that it is a discipline with a history and body of scholarship. Du Cille's complaint regarding African American studies speaks to the general problem of multiculturalism: its selectively ignorant exploration, ensuring a general failure of engagement and its appropriation of the Other. These deficiencies reveal not only the ignorance but also the hubris of those who wish to speak for and hence coopt the Other.

As I also learned in the Georgia episode, the political advantages of multiculturalism are significant. While students learn little regarding the languages, literatures, histories, or philosophies of other cultures, administrators and faculty can pretend that they all have somehow confronted alterity. If you add texts to the curriculum marked by "otherness," then you have provided a nonthreatening element of diversity, without having to engage *real* diversity. Multiculturalism as practiced in universities and colleges in the States today feeds institutional and individual desire for engagement and fosters the pretense that academic criticism can function as a political act. It supports the myth, common to poststructuralist theory, that textual culture can replace activist culture (Ahmad

1992:1). A discourse of freedom, individuality, and tolerance sustains cultural ignorance (Srivastava 1995:16), while the multiculturalist critic aspires to appear relevant on a global level. In this process, the real world and the variety of its literatures are eclipsed by the larger professional hegemonic project.

Some Americans of color have learned to deconstruct such strategies of personal and professional development. There are those who recognize that fragmentary and acontextual representations of ethnic identity are promoted by an intellectual and administrative mainstream out of a deep cynicism regarding the Other as a fossilized object of clinical experimentation. Indeed, multiculturalism has been condemned as a patently deceptive and self-serving upper-class democratization (Fox-Genovese 1986:142), providing a situation governed by a seemingly inclusionary logic of pluralism that only preserves the status quo (Okada 2002:198). It has been recognized as fostering a discredited form of scholarship and canon formation. Nevertheless, the field of literary studies has embraced the ethnicity paradigm by promoting the teaching of the multiethnic literatures of the United States. The political benefits are just too great. Multiculturalists can attempt to grasp the transhistorical similarities of what is perceived as American culture *and* engage in the essentialism of basing their vision of American culture on an overly apologetic and reactionary ethnicity paradigm. Werner Sollors, the white senior African Americanist in a pre-Gates Harvard, subscribed to this universalist interpretation in which race is presented as merely one aspect of ethnicity. One attains status through achievement and identity by descent with the ensuing free play of polarities.[16]

However, there is a significant problem with this vision of race: it supports inferential racism. A series of racist premises and propositions and a set of unquestioned assumptions enter into the construction of the ethnicist model and its neutralized representation of events and situations. Such assumptions allow racist statements to be formulated without any awareness of the racist predicates upon which they are grounded. Let us take, for example, the case of *American Literature,* the ninth volume of *The New Pelican Guide to English Literature.* As San Juan has shown, the chapter of this volume dedicated to Native American literary production is extraordinary. It is filled with quotes ranging from Pound, Ginsburg, Whitman, Rimbaud, Cassirer, Breton, and Rabelais. Native American writers are named only at the end of the chapter (Ford 1988). No specific reference is made to genocide and the continued disposition of American Indians (San Juan 1991:223). Essentially, what we have in this volume is a pretense of inclusion cloaking continued exclusion. In fact, this volume offers something even worse than the customary exclusion of an earlier age. It presents a type of dumbed-down ethnicity-oriented scholarship that pretends to take seriously underrepresented cultures while providing less information regarding them than when they were largely excluded from the canon. Such scholarship offers a more subtly constructed hegemonic vision of race, one that has been codified in textbook form as a valid pedagogic approach.

From a marketing standpoint, it is not only the fragmentary and irresponsibly incomplete representation of minority populations within syllabi that is necessary, but the presence of minority faculty is also important. However, their inclusion into the teaching ranks is less significant than their presence "doing minority things." Once credentialed, one's cosmetic purpose diminishes exponentially if one's teaching and publications do not capitalize on one's gender and ethnicity. A black female junior faculty member who wrote her dissertation on Lully is not permitted to teach French Baroque opera but "encouraged" to teach Scott Joplin. Some minority faculty have been known to get uppity, expecting to teach courses in fields where they have trained. This, too, has been managed, thanks to multiculturalism. If an institution can fill its quotas with minority multiculturalists, it need not recruit minorities in underrepresented (i.e., traditional) fields. One need only make the minimal effort to pass muster as an institution valuing diversity. It is of primary importance that the people of color be given jobs in fields that deal with minority issues because the minority hire exists to showcase not only the institution's commitment to hire people of color but also its commitment to minority programs. Behind the dual role imposed on minority hires (to be a person of color and "do the minority thing"), there is the deep cynicism of institutions regarding the minority instructor's ability to perform in traditional disciplines where they cannot rely on ethnicity-specific intuitive knowledge. Multiculturalism allows universities to balkanize minority professionals under the guise of inclusion. The multiculturalist supplants ethnic minorities whose fields of expertise do not reflect and publicize their ethnicity. In some instances, curricular multiculturalism allows universities to showcase their commitment to minority studies without even having to promote minority hiring.

MASKING THE METANARRATIVE OF RACE

If one cannot be a minority in American universities today, one must find a way to identify with a minority situation. This strategy is dictated less by genuine curiosity than by the fact that universities are motivated by marketing concerns. Marketing in this context is twofold. First, there is marketing to and through university administrators and deans who buy into the idea that multicultural initiatives are the most advanced and "logical" approach to the third world and the miasma of competing ethnicities. Multiculturalism easily degenerates into the diversity of college catalogs, state- or corporate-managed United Colors of Benetton pluralism (Shohat and Stam 2003:6). It assuages institutional needs to recruit and restructure with supposedly cutting-edge responses to new socioeconomic realities. Administrators can pad their score-cards with curricular diversity, even if their institutions maintain an abysmal record in real diversity. Second, the multicultural context allows individual academics to emerge as luminaries in the theoretical/critical pantheon. They then market themselves as theoretical stars and the university markets them, in turn, to attract students and grant money.

Contrary to what multicultural initiatives might suggest, the third world defies packaging, especially by a cadre of cynical professors and administrators seeking the political engagement that they and their institutions never quite achieved in more propitious times. Multiculturalism, claiming to offer a viable mechanism for adjustments of power within historically white-dominated societies, merely serves a cosmetic purpose. While some might pretend that it is a workable model for civic tolerance in societies struggling to free themselves from the burden of their white supremacist past (Hutcheon and Richmond 1990), others view it as a willfully aestheticizing discourse that inadvertently serves to disguise persistent racial tensions. In affecting a respect for the other as a reified object of cultural difference, multiculturalism deflects attention away from social issues such as discrimination, unequal access, and hierarchies of ethnic privilege that are far from being resolved (Huggan 2000:126).

Multiculturalism does not really help those for whom it purports to speak. While affirming the virtues of the margins, it leaves the centers of power uncontested (Gitlin 1995:236). It claims to offer the putative end of metanarratives: all kinds of representations and cultures are deemed as valid as others (Lyotard 1979). However, as Rey Chow notes, multiculturalism still only offers a one-way street. Some form of white culture is the one recognizing the nonwhite culture. In order "to be" or "speak out," the nonwhite culture must seek legitimacy and recognition from white culture and use the language of white culture to produce itself (Rizvi 1994:63). Multiculturalism is really about assimilation with domesticating egalitarian demands attached. In this respect, it follows the corporate model of diversity management. It also obscures issues of power and privilege; it deals with differences by making them tokenistic (Chow 2002:113).

Multiculturalism arose in an attempt to uncover occluded and submerged identities and to liberate the repressed through the dissemination of peoples' histories. Its project was to redraw the boundaries and affirm the authority of internal colonies. The process became fetishized into a cult of ethnicity that seeks to unmask and repudiate inferential racism. However, by promoting a showcase tolerance of diverse ethnic practices, multiculturalism can also be seen as a strategy of an academic elite seeking to displace, diffuse, and thus intensify class, gender, and racial contradictions. The case can be made that the culturalist abuse of ethnicity serves to mask hegemonic domination under the pretext of pluralist tolerance (San Juan 1992:15) or valorize differences to guarantee sameness (San Juan 1995:237). Class divisions and systemic inequalities remain intact.

The reality is that authentic multiculturalism remains the unassimilable welter of incommensurabilities that one finds in the high-tech consultancies and spice emporia on the Buford Highway in Atlanta and Northern Boulevard in Queens. This clash of technological innovation with prosaic reality produces a chaos that cannot be homogenized or coated with a theoretical veneer. The postmodern critiques of racism that we will investigate in the following chapters examine how representative works and subjects are constituted by power and imbricated in the material practice of discourses and institutional structures. They provide the new "isms" to fill the void once the verities of multiculturalism have been totally discredited. What concerns me is that the production of a new round of relevancy is, perhaps, the only essential point in the game. The evolution of postcolonial theory as a critical field supports this anxiety.

CHAPTER 3

POSTCOLONIAL CRITICISM
AND IDENTITARIAN POLITICS

DEFINITIONS AND THE
SCOPE OF POSTCOLONIAL CRITICISM

An initial reading of postcolonial theory highlights the extent to which it is deeply concerned with the location of the theorist, while woefully vague regarding the "location" of the very term *postcoloniality* itself. In fact, a curious situation emerges when we seek to answer the seemingly simple question, what is postcolonialism? Upon investigation of the critical literature, we realize that there is no clear consensus among practitioners themselves as to what constitutes the approach to reading texts from a postcolonial theoretical perspective or even what constitutes the canon of criticism. There is little one can do with definitions that claim postcolonial criticism "covers all the cultures effected by the imperial process from the moment of colonization to the present day" (Ashcroft, Griffiths, and Tiffin 1995:2) or that it "foregrounds a politics of opposition and struggle, and problematizes the key relationship between centre and periphery" (Mishra and Hodge 1991:399).

An essentialism has beset discussions of postcoloniality from its arrival on the critical scene in the 1980s, in the aftermath of Said's own monolithic and essentializing critique of Orientalism. In his magisterial work, *Orientalism* (1978), Said showed how knowledge concerning the Orient was constituted and derived directly from received systems of knowledge already in practice in nineteenth-century Europe. Said sensitized readers to the practices of Europeans who were in a position to construct knowledges and identities of non-Europeans. He did not, however, propose a new methodology or epistemology devoted to elucidating its objects. In fact, Said showed an extraordinary indifference to the diversity of colonial experiences of those areas that might have had a colonization prior to the nineteenth century (Harootunian 2002:152). Even in *Culture and Imperialism* (1993), Said continued to harmonize alternatives and flatten out contradictions in his investigation of the diaspora's relationship to imperial geography. It is precisely this essentialism, this flattening out of the colonial experience into a monolithic process of Orientalism, that Said bequeathed to subsequent postcolonialists.

It comes, therefore, as no surprise that the editors of the theoretical anthology *The Empire Writes Back* include under the rubric of postcolonial literature all literature written in English by societies affected by colonialism, a vast geographical zone including Africa, Australia, Bangladesh, Canada, India, Malaysia, New Zealand, Pakistan, Singapore, the South Pacific Islands, and Sri Lanka. Even the literature of the United States is deemed postcolonial. While it is acknowledged that they all possess "special and distinctive regional characteristics," the authors of this anthology tend to focus on their alleged common experience, a single common condition called the "postcolonial condition" or "postcoloniality," when "they all emerged from the experience of colonialization and asserted themselves by foregrounding the tension with imperial power" (Ashcroft, Griffiths, and Tiffin 1989:2). Another instance of this leveling out process can be seen in the fact that so much of postcolonial theory is associated with the British literature of India. Specifically, the national or ethnic metonyms in postcolonial criticism have migrated to Bengal, which has been made to serve as the model not only for the Indian subcontinent,[1] but also for the entire postcolonial world. A number of leading theorists are Indians, whose initial training was in English studies.[2] Thanks to this demographic, the trope of relations between the colonizer and the colonized in most postcolonial criticism is typified by the putative relationship between the English colonizer and the Bengali subject, conceived according to Hegel's description of the master and the bondsman (Harootunian 2002:168). Also, because its theorists arose from the ranks of English studies, postcolonial criticism encourages us to read the world in translation and in terms of its cultural products, most notably, the novel. The emphasis of literary cultural analysis thus discounts the canon of historical and social scientific inquiry. Sovereignty is invested in readers of the English novel dealing with the imperial geography of late capitalism. In fact, Homi Bhabha and Benedict Anderson make the claim that writing the nation was inconceivable without appealing to novelistic narration. Postcolonial critics thus recuperate the privilege of culture in the most traditional form of English studies, a field of inquiry in which they initially trained and from which they have never really strayed. Other genres, foreign or indigenous, have no equivalent valence.

Postcolonial theory blurs geographical boundaries, overdetermines the role of the English novel, and collapses chronologies. It encompasses the historical beginnings of colonialism with its aftermaths (McClintock 1992:87).[3] Such inconsistencies and methodological eccentricities, however, are largely occluded by the reluctance on the part of the critical milieu in which postcolonial theorizing has developed to define its operations. When definitions appear, they are constructed by editors of anthologies or secondary interpreters of key theorists who never interrogate the methods, ideology, and disciplinary politics that mandate the refusal to define postcolonial criticism in any clear or unambiguous way.[4]

Part of the reason for this seeming lack of clarity may be postcolonial theory's indebtedness to postmodernist literary theory, and, particularly, its tropes of irony, allegory, doubleness, and reduction of everything to metanarratives of contingency and indeterminacy (San Juan 1998:24). Another rationale for this ambiguity may be postcolonial criticism's affinities with poststructual philosophy, especially its rejection of stable identities, fixed meanings, and grounding in universal principles of any sort (Larsen 2000:141). Moreover, poststructuralism has bequeathed to postcolonialism a set of conceptual moves that allow ambivalence to be recast as an emancipatory drama with radical players and stakes (Larsen 2000:15). After all, the very use of the prefix *post* in postcolonialism emblematizes a dynamics of cultural resistance (Hutcheon 1995:10). It has been enough for postcolonial critics to claim they are engaged in unmasking, demystifying, and deconstructing themes of citizenship and the modern state as permanent, transhistorical, and ubiquitous. Beyond such claims, does it really matter what is actually being done? Even when critics appear to question the trajectory of postcolonial criticism, the interrogation often appears as a further exercise in theoretical obfuscation.

The critic Stephen Slemon has asked: "Why are the attributes of postcolonial criticism so widely contested in contemporary usage, and its strategies and sites structurally dispersed?" (Slemon 1995:7). Slemon offered two reasons for this apparent inability within the field to define its parameters. Either postcolonialism's meaning and moment should be read as the disciplinary manifestation of an intellectual paralysis in a cultural and critical moment that might have been, or it represents a display of intellectual vitality in the production of new and diverse interventionary practices, new modes of resistance and representation, and new spaces for the formation of coalitional transformations. One might well suspect this formulation of the problem and counter its assessment by suggesting that the components of the equation have been misidentified. Although it is fashionable to speak in terms of "intervention" and "resistance," such terminology refers to no political or social reality.

The critic then is essentially asking us to judge postcolonial theory in terms of its purely rhetorical gestures. Perhaps a critical moment has not been lost. It is even possible that we do not have a diversity of opinion regarding postcolonialism that is really vital. What is, perhaps, most interesting is the "prematurely celebratory" (McClintock 1992:87) tone of such a formulation and the seeming nonchalance it exhibits for postcolonial criticism's ahistoricity and universalizing deployments (Shohat 1992:99).

HISTORY AND POSTCOLONIAL SUBJECTIVITY

The manner in which the argument has been framed betrays not only the fundamental presuppositions that inform postcolonial criticism but also the parameters of its discourse and the theoretical situation out of which they arose. The critical task of postcolonial criticism has been aestheticized to such a degree that demands for rationality are portrayed as symptoms of the malaise that postcolonial critics claim to combat. We have seen how postcolonialism's critical precursors established the parameters of its discourse. Structuralism valorized a need for systems and devalorized history. Lévi-Strauss revealed that exceptions and inconsistencies could be irrelevant to meaning once some overarching structure had been established. Foucault explained how discourse is centered on power relationships and social materiality is always imbricated with power. Said's *Orientalism* showed the extent to which the Other was monolithically constructed to support imperial hegemony. Lacan offered a psychoanalytic justification for the mobility of location. Derrida and de Man cautioned us to distrust facts. Postcolonial theory also has been informed by studies in nationalism (Anderson), third-world allegory (Jameson),[5] subaltern historiography (Guha, Chatterjee, Prakash), earlier anticolonial theory (Césaire, Fanon, Memmi), and the musings of postcolonial theorists themselves (Said, Spivak, Bhabha) (Shohat and Stam 2003:13). With the exception of Spivak's Mahasweta Devi, vernacular texts tend not to enter into discussion,[6] since the postcolonial archive usually consists of a limited body of published texts in English, the official language of intellectual power at the late-imperial center (Clark 1996:24), as if it were exclusively representative. Postcolonial criticism thus does not demand linguistic skills or the tools of an archivist. The archive is largely metaphorical anyway.

Postcolonial criticism invites cross-cultural analysis without demanding extensive cultural knowledge. It trades in stereotypes and the fantasy of locating a genuine anticolonial nationalistic subject grasped through a psychoanalytic framework that is itself not culturally specific (Harootunian 2002:172).[7] This lack of specificity has led some critics to compare the discourse of postcolonial criticism with that of colonial thinking (Shohat 1992:99). Postcolonial theory still orients the globe according to a single binary of Western historicism (McClintock 1992:85). It marks and markets the multitudinous cultures of the world and telescopes their geopolitical distinctions into invisibility (McClintock 1992:86). One colonial experience can come to resemble another. The critics indiscriminately embrace the Other and level out the various competing Others. What is important is that the Other always be perceived as correct, regardless of differences. It must fulfill the critic's desire for a pure otherness in pristine luminosity (Chow 1995:45). In this manner, postcolonial criticism exhibits a banal Rousseauism that privileges non-Western culture and glories in its presumptive eventual resurgence as it topples some establishment (Clark 1996:44).

The most sustained complaint against postcolonial criticism, however, is that it claims historical method without a grasp of historical facts. As Aijaz Ahmad (1992) has shown, if you level out all histories, you can take up a thousand available microhistories arbitrarily since they all amount more or less to the same thing. Relying on the experience of modern colonialism, the critic divides history into manageable and isolated segments while at the same time arguing against the false homogenization of Orientalist projects (Bahri 1995:52). Ahmad bewails the postcolonial theorist's denial of history, especially the histories of peoples, their trajectories of survival, and their achievements. For example, the "historical" narrative of Said's *Culture and Imperialism* is quite abstract, consisting more of textual commentary and literary history than history, per se. Bhabha even vaunts the antihistoricism in his rewriting of the nation as narration. By mystifying the political effects of Western postmodern hegemony, frameworks such as Bhabha's cult of linguistic and psychological ambivalence and Spivak's metaphysics of textualism further obscure the history of peoples' resistance to imperialism.

This lack within postcolonial criticism of any effective historical consciousness explains why it has primarily found urgent currency in the first world and few ripples resonate in the excolonized worlds of South Asia and Africa. The predominance of critical contestants in Euroamerican centers reflects how much this theory is inherently Eurocentric and culture bound (Clark 1996:24). Critics of postcolonial theory have begun to question the agendas lurking behind its rhetoric and its complicity with certain forms of Eurocentric cultural theory (Radhakrishnan 1993:750) and the power struggles replicated within this critical discourse. It is, indeed, ironic the degree to which postcolonial theory depends on European cultural theory while, at the same time, claiming that European knowledge can never disclose the truth regarding the colonized (San Juan 2002:259).

Following Lyotard, only the local narratives can have validity. The task then becomes for the critic to uncover in the "native" narrative what has been lost in the voicelessness of the colonial subject. The theorists, "assorted Australian, Indian and Canadian ventriloquists," must then speak for "speechless subalterns" (San Juan 1998:30). Their need to mediate stems from the notion, common to most poststructural theory, that some heritage of systems limits the reader. Our present condition, although seemingly benign, imposes an existential limit, and theory alone can liberate us from systemic constraints (Fluck 1996:216). In this respect, postcolonial criticism once again reveals its indebtedness to Foucault in its lavish declarations of resistance. Missing in all these discussions of power and theory as a political act is any inquiry into how the text's appearance as a network of hegemonic or subversive gestures suits the state of literary theoretical professionalization or how this cooptation reflects the critics' class interests as bourgeois intellectuals ensconced in metropolitan institutions. Theory thus allows individuals cut off from any effective social action and buoyed by their security as academic professionals to coopt the voices of and claim solidarity with the disenfranchised. The theorist's alien- ation from *real* powerlessness (as in the case of the academic Marxist's guilt vis-à-vis the worker) is then replaced by a posture of powerlessness vis-à-vis representation. The critic must self-fashion him- or herself through imaginary marginalization resulting in the wide-ranging identification of a privileged class of academics with the marginalized Other. I have termed this process a "brahminization of theory" and will examine it more closely in the next chapter. The historically oppressed become the new role models for the critic. In this way, theory and professionalism interact and justify each other (Fluck 1990:18). Postcolonial criticism may well aspire to decenter Enlightenment discourse and repudiate Eurocentric models. The sad truth of the matter is, however, that this process of "expressive individualism" (Fluck 1996:227) only seems to liberate the critic.

THE POSTCOLONIAL CRITIC

This positioning of postcolonial critics has not gone unnoticed. Neil Larsen (2000) has analyzed their theoretical inconsistencies. Benita Parry, claiming that they have suppressed native voices, has chided them for the exorbitation of their roles. The theorization of subalternity, she notes, "gives no speaking part to the colonized, effectively writing out the evidence of native agency recorded in India's two-hundred year struggle against British conquest and the Raj" (Parry 1987:35). Arif Dirlik (1997:343) and Rajeswari Sunder Rajan (1997:598) have cited the postcolonial theorists' disengagements from significant issues of neocolonialism and retreat into a rarified form of postmodern abstraction. In particular, Dirlik has challenged the fetishism of notions such as hybridity and postcolonialism's antirevolutionary motivations. Dirlik has also commented on postcolonialism's emergence as a form of global capitalism where critics, commanding high salaries in the first world, presume to be existentially connected to continuing problems of third-world social, political, and cultural domination. He criticizes postcolonial criticism's failure to take into account Asian participation in the unfolding discourse of the Orient (Dirlik 1997:118). Dirlik concludes that postcolonial discourse is not so much an expression of agony over identity for the third-world intellectuals who have arrived in first-world academe (as it is often made to appear), as it is a manifestation of their newfound power (Dirlik 1994:329, 339, 356).

Aijaz Ahmad (1992) charges that the categories of "postcolonial" or "third-world" literatures are wholly products of metropolitan and first-world institutions (universities, publishing houses). In the chapter entitled "Languages of Class, Ideologies of Immigrations" of *In Theory,* he sketched the history of postcolonial studies as resulting from the integration of intellectuals from Asia, Africa, and Latin America into North American and Western European intellectual and academic establishments. Ahmad characterized these scholars as a small academic elite who knows it will not return home. They join a faculty, frequent the circuits of conferences and the university presses, and develop, often with the greatest degree of personal innocence and missionary zeal, quite considerable stakes in overvalorizing what has already been designated as "Third World Literature" (Ahmad 1992:85). Said's construct of postcolonial hybridity becomes a celebration of the postcolonial intellectual as the true hero of cultural anti-imperialism, fighting behind the lines in metropolitan theaters. Larsen seconds Ahmad's judgment claiming that Said appears self-serving and elitist when he asserts, "In a totally new way in Western culture, the interventions of non-European artists and scholars cannot be dismissed or silenced, and these interventions are not only an integral part of a political movement, but in many ways the movement's successfully guiding imagination, intellectual and figurative energy reseeing and rethinking the terrain common to whites and non-whites" (Said 1993:212; cited in Larsen 2000:153–54). Where Dirlik recognizes no programmatic politics in postcolonial theory (Dirlik 1997:66), Ahmad sees its transhistoricity as an ideological alibi to expunge determinate histories and release postcolonial subjects from any bonds of accountability. It is precisely postcolonialism's complicity with the status quo that has received the most sustained critique at the hands of these critics and others (Callinicos, Eagleton) (San Juan 2002:274–75). No matter how often elite academics offer Foucauldian genealogical excavations

(Prakash, Chatterjee), existing property relations and asymmetries of actual power relations in places such as India (class, gender, local religion) remain untouched (San Juan 2002:259).

The disconnect between postcolonial theory and any critical claims to a practical reform agenda may account for the theorists' refusal to define postcolonial theory in an unambiguous manner. In this interpretation, the lack of clarity regarding the nature of postcolonial theory might well not necessarily point to diversity or vitality, as Slemon so ingenuously suggested, but rather a tacit understanding on the part of the critics that their projects are nothing but games of identity. Any analysis of the literature of postcolonial criticism highlights the extent to which the intellectual rigor and development of the analysis are seriously circumscribed by ideological posturing, reifying critical jargon and strategies of self-representation. It might well be that postcolonial criticism never intended to address the myriad problems of analyzing third-world societies but rather the structures of power and, by extension, the critic's position vis-à-vis these structures. The logic of this type of postcolonial criticism reaches its natural conclusion, then, when a text is only a text and refers to no historical action.[8] No coloniality, no postcoloniality—just ruminations on fantasies of power. Postcolonial studies of this genre strike an old-fashioned pose of the European psychoanalyst who unmasks the cultural crime of deformation. They are based on the virtually self-explanatory phenomenon of cultural struggle and adjustment.

Not only is postcolonial theory dislocated from any real praxis, but it is also disengaged from what has preceded it. Since the postcolonial critic posits him or herself as someone with access to positional knowledge, the work of generations of nonpostcolonial scholars (Orientalists, those who fit only marginally into the construction of Orientalism, and others who made a genuine effort to bring cultures formerly called "Oriental" into the Euro-American continuum) can be overlooked. Often, given the narrow formation of the postcolonial critic, he/she is unaware that a body of scholarship written by area specialists pertaining to a given topic even exists. The absence of any traditional *Forschungsbericht*[9] is justified, since the postcolonial critic can dismiss earlier work as serving a decrepit ideology (Clark 1996:23). There is, of course, a self-serving component to any charges of ideology evident also in the quasimessianic manner in which the critic positions him/herself to speak exclusively for the Other. Since Spivak's subalterns theoretically are mute, she can effectively coopt their voice. In the process, she creates a need for the theorist (Spivak herself) who will determine and monopolize the discourse of the victimized. This is, indeed, a slippery game. The postcolonial critic, laboring the notions of voicelessness and absence, serves to license the neglect of any texts ("archives," "voices," and "spaces") that contradict a postcolonial theoretical script.

All this subterfuge would be fine and good were it not for the fact that rhetorical engagement poses as a blueprint for social change, especially for critics "exiled" from the native sites they propose to analyze. It is true that the location of critics does not necessarily diminish their message, just as being rooted to the territory of one's origin does not assure a "pure and authentic standpoint" (Michel 1995:87). The problem is one of representation. Autominoritized (note: not necessarily minority) subjects should not blithely assume roles as spokespersons for minority communities. Regardless of their own socioeconomic status and privileges, they should not speak as or for minorities and as representatives for a minority community and its victimization. They should not function as "victims in proxy" (Bahri 1995:73). When they do, they should be seriously challenged.

Spivak herself, on occasion, voices concern that some critics might lack the objectivity to conceptualize their *Dasein*, as if by projection she is absolved of accruing any blame herself. She also worries that we as teachers are "becoming complicitous in the perpetuation of a new orientalism, given the proliferation of job listings in Third World literature" that she, her students (and all of us) benefit from (Spivak 1993:56; cited in Chow 2002:113). She clearly sees herself as an agent of resistance to such occurrences. Nevertheless, despite her self-blandishments, she acknowledges that third-world–born critics can fall into the trap of becoming native informants. She stops short, however, of blaming herself for engaging in "revolutionary tourism" and the "celebration of testimony" (Spivak 1993:284), terms she herself has coined, projected onto others, and her Indian-based critics have applied to her. Her slippery position as a critic allows her to claim to inhabit a culture of imperialism and criticize it from within.[10] Spivak's strategy of projection, utilized by Said with such aplomb, masks a multitude of sins. Said had a penchant for stereotyping those whom he had accused of stereotyping others. In a similar fashion, postcolonial criticism is consistently guilty of what it claims to repudiate. With Said and Spivak, mystification and moralism go hand in hand. No one seems terribly bothered by the fact that victimization by proxy represents false consciousness.

The concept of the "margin versus the center" in postcolonial criticism allows the critic to theorize always from the impregnable position of "the margin" but also invoke "ambiguity," "binarism," and "splitting" as constitutive of that margin and those that inhabit it. Bhabha's ambivalence arises out of poststructuralism's "difference of writing" that informs any cultural performance and is found in certain privileged positionalities and experiences, especially in postcolonialism's migration narratives of the cultural and political diaspora. Bhabha's "poetics of exile" (Bhabha 1994:5) allows the theorist to not be constrained to "stand" on particular ground or take up a position, but instead to "slide ceaselessly" (Bhabha 1990:300) in liminal space that is full of irony and aporiae. Bhabha makes marginality analogous to the arbitrary position of the signifier. Following Lacan, the signifier is constantly suspended in a chain that never connects with the signified and is forever caught in perpetual slippage because of differential temporalities and spaces that resist comprehensive explanations.

With such concepts as "ambivalence," "hybridity," and "third space of negotiation," Bhabha brings deconstructionist theories, antiessentialism, and Lacanian theories of subjectivity into postcolonial criticism. His notion of hybridity and its liminality provides a place from which to speak both of and as the minority, the exilic, the marginal, and the emergent (Bhabha 1990:300). Both Bhabha and Spivak occlude historical determinacy by deploying psychoanalytic and linguistic frameworks that take market relations for granted. In Bhabha's work, Foucault is invoked to establish the disequilibrium of the modern state and Bhabha's conception of the marginality of the "people." Said and Bhabha accept Foucault's dubious claim that the most individualized group in modern society are the marginals, yet to be integrated into the political reality. They attempt to validate interpretation from the margin, where third-world intellectuals and metropolitan culture position exiled figures as the most authoritative voices. Said's and Spivak's self-conscious privileging of global metropolitan culture excludes those without access to metropolitan centers. As Ahmad noted, the "Orient" is consumed in the form of those fictions of this world available in bookshops in metropolitan countries (Ahmad 1992:217). Said, in particular, positions the "migrant" or "traveler" as "our model for academic freedom" (cited in Krishnaswamy 1995:127), hence his desire to automigrant himself in biographical accounts. Once the need for a "tribe of interpreters" (Bhabha 1990:253) has been established, migrant/traveler critics can then set out on their anointed mission as the "translators of the dissemination of texts and discourses across cultures" (Bhabha 1990:293).

Traveling theory requires, among other things, "a kind of 'doubleness' in writing; a temporality of representation that moves between cultural formations and social processes without a 'centered' causal logic" (Bhabha 1990:293). Here, Said, Spivak, and Bhabha can be "located" at a place where theorists are necessary to interpret across cultures and academic disciplines without the inconvenience of having to pinpoint cultural particularities. The rationale has now been created for the theorist to say whatever he or she likes, the only constraint or test of validity being that the proper cultural space is occupied and that the writing validates and promotes the ambiguity and contradictoriness of this position. The critic's location, it seems, always overrides the national historical situation and exegetical context.

The personal search on the part of the critic might be interpreted as masking a lack of calling or significance. The stakes are considerable: personal validation within an incestuously boundaried field, among other critics deemed worthy of making the call. Ashis Nandy was harsh but insightful when he described them as "circus-trained opponents" and "tragic counterplayers performing their last gladiator-like acts of courage in front of appreciative Caesars" (Nandy 1983:xiv). The authoritative critic has carefully picked through information provided by native informants and provides the dominant voice. Although postcolonial critics claim acuity vis-à-vis the intricacies in readings (Sunder Rajan 1997:603–05), their ignorance of key aspects in the narrative they seek to deconstruct can lead to gross distortions. However, these mistakes are neither given significance nor, for that matter, acknowledged in service of the overriding importance assigned to the critic's theoretical script. The Other is eclipsed by the critic's conception of it—a conception whose major function is to validate the theorist within the community of theorists. The intellectual quest is thus bound up in the idealized image of the critic's own theory or theory itself as an ideal. This is a new solipsism as well as an aestheticization of the critical project in "criticism for criticism's sake." Criticism has become, then, the language game among theorists, and there are professional benefits to be had from "syndicated oppositionality" (Huggan 2001:9).

It is my belief that postcolonial criticism places desire on the level of the critic's need for validation. The third-world critic somehow should be uniquely positioned not only to explicate but also to understand realities. Third-world reality can be "bracketed" before the argument begins, since the critic's primary interest lies in structuring it thematically for a milieu that consumes these structures. Critics usually do not question how their professional lives replicate the structures on which imperialism was based and functioned. There is no acknowledgment that postcolonial criticism might appear anachronistic (Larsen 2000). In their talk of the rupture of decolonization, critics tend to ignore the fact that they are not writing in the 1950s (Behdad 2000:82).

The date may be long past for criticism to have social impact. So now, criticism has built the whole critical project as an investigation of sociopolitical impotence. Where does potency lie? It resides only in the critic's relationship to colleagues, only in the critical milieu, in the coining and usage of jargon as an exercise in pyrotechnics. At the imperial center, postcolonial theory enables those who come from cultures formerly under colonialism's direct sway to speak back (Clark 1996:23). The dexterity of language manipulation garners the critic points in the rarefied linguistic contest. In this respect, Spivak remains the undisputed master. Her deconstructive tour de force, *A Critique of Postcolonial Reason* (1999) demands careful translation to discover that, after promises of insight, originality, and depth, the real goal of the inquiry remains always the same: the valorization of the third-world critic installed in a major metropolitan university in the West who provides the most authentic voice.

The above-mentioned posture of self-criticism provides a common thread in the late criticism of postcolonialism. It masks any true analyses of the critics' actual positions or the position of the field in global capitalist networks (Hall 1996). As we have noted, here too, Spivak sets the standard. In *A Critique of Postcolonial Reason,* she peppers her discussions on Kant, Marx, and Bangladesh child labor abuses with disclaimers regarding the significance of her enterprise that experienced readers have learned to recognize as a ruse to disarm her critics. But this posture of concerned critics always challenging their motives and projects is fairly commonplace. Christopher L. Miller (1998), questioning the rigid ideological tropes that inform postcolonial criticism, warns of our need to eschew absolutes. However, his seeming willingness to examine postcolonialism's stratagems, like Spivak's, never extends far beyond rhetorical gestures. In *Islands and Exiles* (1998), Chris Bongie grappled with the paralysis he experienced vis-à-vis the incommensurabilities of the postcolonial situation. No theorist is damned, no theorist deemed worthy of apotheosis. Everything points to a middle ground, a slippery site including what is loathed and what is loved. All the essentialisms of the precolonial and the colonial past are harshly criticized but cannot be done away with because they still embody a reality that is deeply embedded in the present.

Postcolonial criticism's elision of class, psychologisms, and reduction of large-scale political struggles to an intrapsychic ahistoricism is, indeed, dubious, as is the critic's ambiguous relationship to ethnic studies and the study of indigenous peoples (Shohat and Stam 2003:15). This is a critical school that flagellates itself with rhetorical self-doubt and claims to torture itself with constant self-evaluation when, in fact, it exhibits a consistent lack of true self-reflection. Postcolonial critics spend little time actually considering their role in the "micropolitics of the academy" (Rabinow 1986:252–53). It is sufficient to claim openness to the universal dimension of the culture of our time and thereby be able to situate oneself in this world and analyze its contradictions, while simultaneously being able to remain in living and close communion with the popular classes and share their history (Amin 1990:136; cited in Lazarus 1999:142). This paradox goes unquestioned. It is quite indicative that the intelligentsia on the periphery is not defined by the class origin of its members. The privileging of the voice of third-world immigrants is not based on their status as members of exploited classes but merely on their ideological espousal of anticapitalism. Even the term *anticapitalist* overdignifies an antinormative adversarial posturing since these critics show no clear understanding of how economic processes work, but rather exhibit a childish and instinctive rejection of traditions and institutions.

Nor does the late theory of postcolonialism question why so much attention is paid to the trio of Said, Spivak, and Bhabha. The very existence of such a hierarchy of thinkers calls to mind Bourdieu's notion of cultural capital—that the literary field is a site of struggle in which what is at stake is the power to impose a dominant definition of the writer/critic and thereby delimit the population of those authorized to call themselves writers. They assume the task of consecrating both the producers and products, whether these take the form of prefaces for volumes, reviews of scholarship, textbook editing, or so on (Bourdieu 1993:42). This restrictive number of "name-brand critics" has become more important than the field itself (Loomba 1998:xv). I would even venture to claim that these critics *are* the field itself. What is there to postcolonial criticism, what body of readings is there beyond this handful of reedited articles? The "alterity industry" is a self-enclosed affiliative network whose validity consists of cross-referencing each other. Students do not challenge obtuse articles because they themselves lack any expertise in colonial and postcolonial histories and cultures (Loomba 1998:xvi; cited in Huggan 2001:259).

The significant point here is that there is very little serious concern with the validity of the postcolonial project voiced by its practitioners. Throughout the criticism, we hear echoes of Slemon's pretense that something terribly vital has been occurring in these discussions. Bongie (1998), for his part, affects a subdued optimism that new perspectives will develop, social situations will change, and new writers will discover the path out of the theoretical mire. However, it has now become clear that we are not waiting for Godot but keeping the faith until Lohengrin arrives.

THE REPRESSIVE ALLURE OF POSTCOLONIAL CRITICISM

No matter how much these critics obscure the continuities and discontinuities of colonial power (McClintock 1992:87–88), little of substance results from the discussions of postcolonialism, hybridity, or subalternity. By reducing the facts of exploitation to the status of discourse and intertextuality, postcolonial criticism minimizes the effects of social subjects shaping their lives. The critical focus on past forms of ideological hegemony enables it to disregard contemporary abuses (Dirlik 1994:356). We do not see in postcolonial criticism any sustained or viable critique of neocolonialism.[11] Postcolonial criticism might even be said to contribute to neocolonialism, since excolonies are yet again used to provide "raw materials" for Western academic consumption (Behdad 2000:82). Postcolonial criticism focuses primarily on the overvalued diasporic intellectual (San Juan 2002:278). It makes no reference to internal colonies such as Puerto Rico, affirmative action, or undocumented aliens. The main problem that postcolonial criticism masks is that of class. Critics, as presumptive ideologues of actual or hypothetical authoritarian and statist regimes, may well be uncomfortable with forces that empower individual actors. The historical evidence unfailingly discloses the complicity of upper classes in reproducing systems of inequalities and brutalities (Larsen 2000:140). Yet postcolonial criticism cleanses the postcolonial subject of both its historical and class determination. In this regard, postcolonial criticism might be seen as abetting and perpetuating structural racism.[12]

Ethnic groups in postcolonial societies rarely enter into discussion, let alone are affected by it (Dirlik 1997:337). In fact, there is no space at all for fourth-world peoples dominated by third-world nations (Shohat 1992:105). In the discursive realm of postcolonial discourse, power and difference between racialized minorities in the metropoles and in the third world disappear. As the librettist for the Broadway show *Bombay Dreams* was quoted several years ago as saying, "Brown is the new black." William Safire noted in the *New York Times* that Meera Syal was not in this instance making a fashion statement. She was alluding rather to the popularity of South Asians in the West. The culture of people with brown skin from South Asia is now "hotter" than that of the culture of black-skinned people in the estimation of "with-it" whites (Safire 2004:18). Indeed, postcolonial politics can be seen as being complicit with late capitalism's drive to maintain its ruthless hegemony over the world's multitudes, especially its people of color (Ahmad 1995b; cited in San Juan 1998:6). The success of postcolonial (PC) theory has been seen in terms of a third-world strategy to contain "pocs" (people of color) (Shohat 1992:105). To a certain degree, PC theory enables educational institutions to contribute to the hegemonic social process reproducing inequality. In the United States, the dominant issue is not colonialism and postcolonialism (as in England and India) but civil rights and post–civil rights (Frankenberg and Mani 1993). Postcolonial criticism glosses over this fact or, indeed, occludes it. Vijay Prashad puts it succinctly: institutions use Indians as a weapon against black America (Prashad 2000:7).

In both the United States and India, affirmative action has hit everyone hard. Across American culture and certainly across Indian caste groups, there is a deep feeling that ground has been lost by those segments of the population who are used to garnering the advantages of privileged status within their respective societies. Whites in America and brahmins in India cannot expect doors to open as easily as in the days prior to affirmative action and the Mandal Commission Report on compensating discrimination. Upper-caste academic displaced persons adopt the minority status of ersatz African Americans. Their willingness to "play the race card" stems, in part, from the complexity of Indian constructions of race and color.[13] Upper-caste Hindus have long sought to use notions of "purity of blood" and "Caucasian features" to exercise power over the majority of the population who have been dubbed the "non-Aryan Untouchables" (Mazumdar 1989:31). The "Aryan myth" in India is much more than a desire on the part of the colonized to be the equal of the colonizer. It is also a myth justifying class hegemony (Mazumdar 1989:32). As Harold Isaacs put it rather bluntly in the 1970s, Indians who see themselves as descendants of the Aryans think of themselves as more white than "whites." "This endows them with a sort of Mayflower status in relation to 'whiteness' or 'Aryanism' which they deny to many of their own darker-skinned countrymen. This India, peculiarly outraged, is not challenging the white man's racism as such. He is crying: 'How dare you assume your air of Aryan superiority over me when I am just as Aryan as you, even more so'" (Isaacs 1972:290). Isaacs claims that this Indian response to American racism—claiming to be white—has existed from the very beginnings of their immigration to these shores. It was first repudiated in the Supreme Court ruling against Bhagat Singh Thind in 1923. Prior to this ruling, dozens of Indian immigrants had gained U.S. citizenship on the basis of their claim to be Caucasian. The Supreme Court ruled that "Caucasian" was not synonymous with "white." The Indians who had thus earned citizenship did not qualify as white people and, as a consequence, lost their citizenship.

Indians' belief in their intrinsic "whiteness" as Aryans has never disappeared. It resurfaced during the main surge in immigration to the States in the late 1960s and early 1970s, reflecting their greater understanding of American racism. Indian immigrants gradually came to recognize the benefits to be accrued through minority status and sought to position themselves for gain of the resources available to historically oppressed minorities. In 1975, the Association of Indians in America (AIA) successfully lobbied to add Indians to the U.S. Census Bureau's nonwhite category (Nomura, Endo, Sumido, et al., 1989:35). They undertook a major campaign for federal government acknowledgment of minority status and the establishment of a separate category listing in the 1980 U.S. Census. Between 1950 and 1975, Indians (along with Pakistanis, Malayans, Thais, and Sri Lankans) were categorized as "other white" and not separately counted in the census. With this ruling, they were now able to gain minority status as nonwhite Caucasians (Mazumdar 1989:35). Vijay Prashad has noted that Indians had come a long way since the days when W. E. B. Du Bois claimed they recoiled from being mistaken for Negroes and forced to share in their disabilities (Du Bois 1985:315; cited in Prashad 2000:157). Prashad evokes Du Bois's question to the blacks: "How does it feel to be a problem?" and asks his fellow Indian Americans, "How does it feel to be a solution?" (Prashad 2000:6). In other words, Indians have effectively become part of the solution to the continued disenfranchisement of minorities within American academe. Like other intellectuals, they may one day have to face up, as Rey Chow has noted, to their fateful relation to those objects of study behind which they hide as voyeurs, as fellow victims, and as self-appointed custodians (Chow 1993:118–19; cited in Clark 1996:24). Ultimately the issue of accountability (Sunder Rajan 1997:606) may call for some reckoning, but that time has not yet come. In the sly politics of othering, the question of who is speaking for whom (San Juan 2002:183) has not yet been answered, although a need for reassessment looms large before the postcolonial critic as it becomes increasingly apparent that the periphery does not appear on its own terms.

While awaiting this reckoning, elites from the excolonial world, possessing a deep sense of self-worth and further legitimized by an Ivy League/Oxbridge education, are "at the ready to step in in the name of affirmative hiring." "Highly commodified distinguished professors" "rack up points" on university administrators' "score card of cultural diversity" (Bahri 1995:71). Postcolonialism is "more palatable and less foreign sounding to skeptical deans than Third World Studies, more global and less fuddy-duddy than Commonwealth Studies" (McClintock 1992:93). Playacting is not inherently evil, except when "academic gestures of acceptance of visible difference presented by displaced Third World postcolonials" mask "the continued disenfranchisement of second and third generational American minorities" (Bahri 1995:71). The theory of the margin provides the rationale and its practitioners the personnel to undermine affirmative action. Ahmad has suggested that colonialisms of the past are, perhaps, less significant than imperialisms of the present (Ahmad 1992:222). As Dirlik has noted, in their very globalism, the cultural requirements of transnational corporations (of which we must count universities) can no longer afford the cultural parochialism of an earlier day. They have a need to internationalize themselves. In academic institutions, this process often takes the form not of promoting scholarship in a conventional sense but of "importing" and "exporting" students and faculty (Dirlik 1994:330, 354–55; cited in Robbins 2000:164).

It is, indeed, ironic that the discourse of decenteredness makes possible the direct transfer of the third-world elites to American elite positions and that the discourse of marginality serves to center these theorists in remunerative posts in the metropolitan center. Agency is arrogated to borderland scholastics seeking to negotiate a zone between the bourgeois comprador nationalism of neocolonized nation-states and the cosmopolitan high culture of the metropole (San Juan 2002:278). It is, therefore, no wonder that postcolonial criticism's "strategies and sites [are] structurally dispersed" (Slemon 1995:7). Postcolonial critics, all deconstructionists of hegemony, have constructed the theoretical priority of the margin (its position as the only authentic voice and its supremacy over any competing voices) in order to establish a location of power from which they themselves most directly benefit.

CHAPTER 4

THE BRAHMINIZATION OF THEORY: COMMODITY FETISHISM AND FALSE CONSCIOUSNESS

Let me try and describe a Westernized Indian woman with whom I ought to have a lot in common and whose company I ought to enjoy. She has been to Oxford or Cambridge or some smart American college. She speaks flawless, easy, colloquial English with a charming lilt of an accent. She has a degree in economics or political science or English literature. She comes from a good family.... How lucky for me if I could have such a person for a friend! What enjoyable, lively times we two could have together!

In fact, my teeth are set on edge if I have to listen more than five minutes—yes, even though everything she says is so true and in line with the most advanced opinions of today. But, when she says it, somehow, even though I know the words to be true, they ring completely false. It is merely lips moving and sounds coming out: it doesn't mean anything, nothing of what she says (though she says it with such conviction, skill, and charm) is of the least importance to her. She is only making conversation in the way she knows educated women have to make conversation. And so it is with all of them.... They know modern India to be an important subject and they have a lot to say about it: but though they themselves *are* modern India, they don't look at themselves, they are not conditioned to look at themselves except with the eyes of foreign experts whom they have been taught to respect. And while they are fully aware of India's problems and are up on all the statistics and all the arguments for and against nationalization and a socialistic pattern of society, all the time it is as if they were talking about some *other* place—as if it were a subject for debate—an abstract subject—and not a live animal actually moving under their feet.

—Ruth Prawer Jhabvala, *Out of India*

INTRODUCTION

In this excerpt from *Out of India,* the novelist Ruth Prawer Jhabvala presents a scathing portrait of a certain type of "Westernized Indian woman." Although this character is alluring and seductive, the narrator is most struck by the feeling of uneasiness she experiences in her company. The narrator claims that although the Indian woman's words appear valid and "in line with the most advanced opinions" of the day, they "ring completely false." This woman might "be India," but she performs an India for others. She constructs an India for the consumption of "foreign experts" whom she has been "taught to respect." I must confess that I suspect that this characterization describes a phenomenon of identity construction that is not limited to the world of fiction. Indeed, the sentiments described by the author in this autobiographical statement remind me of feelings I have experienced reading certain postcolonial critics. The performance sounds serious, erudite, and convincing, but I still feel it is somehow inauthentic, a construct created to be consumed in the West as "India" regardless of the fact that it is radically different from some "other place" that is India.

In "The Fascist Longings in Our Midst," Rey Chow has examined in detail the politics behind academic identity construction. Chow claims that we presently live in a fascist intellectual environment in which facile attitudes, pretentious credentials, and irresponsible work habits are fostered in the name of cultural pluralism (Chow 1995:39). She defines fascism as a form of idealism that causes us to love power and desire the very thing that dominates us (Chow 1995:39). She also offers a Freudian interpretation that views fascism as the projection of a lack. One can, according to André Bazin, transform this lack into a projection of good intentions shining forth in dazzling light (Chow 1995:36), similar to Paul Virilio's concept of 'fascism' as a production of light and luminosity (Chow 1995:37). Chow equates fascism's production of idealism with the projectional production of luminosity as self-evidence. She draws upon Joan Scott's discussion of the privileging of personal experience as a critical weapon against universalisms. Scott argued that personal experience became the uncontestatory evidence, invulnerable to theoretical challenge and the fundamental point of explanation for historical difference. Alternative history now aspires toward the same luminosity, visibility, and self-evidence of the Self's personal experience (Chow 1995:38). To illuminate this point, Chow offers a fictional scenario whose heroine exhibits the power that has been accorded to personal experience as evidence.

Chow tells the "Story of O," a person of color from the third world enrolled in a graduate program in a North American university. Although upper class, "O" pretends to be from poor peasant stock, thus enhancing her cachet as a third-world intellectual. She "muddles and bluffs" her way through her coursework and begins a dissertation on social protest groups among the underclass of her country of origin. For several years she dabbles, doing no serious reading or research but making her presence known by speaking extemporaneously at various conferences. She holds Western capitalism in contempt, brandishes slogans of solidarity with downtrodden classes in the third world, but clearly is determined to "get her fair share of fame, privilege and material well-being in the First World by hook or by crook" (Chow 1995:40). She fakes her way through graduate school; her project exists only in vague generalities she habitually recites, yet she receives unbridled support from well-established academics across the United States, many of whom are white males. Some assert that she is the most brilliant young intellectual they have encountered from the "third world." With such glowing recommendations, she secures a job teaching at a U.S. university. Chow then speculates on the nature of her fictitious heroine's success. She likens it to the mass process described in the classic story of the emperor's new clothes. "By seeing a student of color, no matter how pretentious and fraudulent, as self-evidently correct and deserving of support, these supporters receive an image of *themselves* that is at once enlightenedly humble ('I submit to you, since you are a victim of our imperialism') and beautiful ('Look how decent I am by submitting to you'), and thus eminently gratifying" (Chow 1995:40). Chow's point is that although "O" is the one "cheating her way through the system, she *alone is not to blame for this ridiculous situation*" (Chow 1995:41).

The "flagrantly irresponsible environment of cultural pluralism nurtures her behavior and allows it to thrive" (Chow 1995:41). In the white liberal academy's enthusiasm for "people of color," Chow sees a form of fascism, "an identification with an idealized other placed in a position of unquestionable authority . . . a massive submission to a kind of figure of 'experience' that is assumed to be, to use the terms of Scott's analysis, luminously self-evident" (Chow 1995:41). The object of rebellion is the West or Western imperialism. Persons of color are the figures upon whom such feelings are projected, regardless of their actual political space. As Chow notes, fascism functions here because the "in spite of" is transformed into "precisely because." People see "O" as legitimate and exemplary *precisely because* she is neither. They *themselves* provide the vision that makes up for this lack (Chow 1995:41). She becomes "a cipher, an automaton performing the predictable notions of the 'Third world' intellectual *they* desire" (Chow 1995:42).[1]

The "evidence of experience" allows those who support "persons of color to insult them a second time" (Chow 1995:42). Multicultural and postcolonial initiatives instituted on campuses throughout the United States can contribute to this process in the manner in which their courses are staffed and configured. Multicultural and postcolonial courses and initiatives are particularly suspect if they are funded primarily because first-world intellectuals are overridingly preoccupied with how they themselves can become "other"—by claiming "as little as 1/64th share" of otherness or projecting a scholarly profile of cosmopolitanism through publications purportedly dealing with global, transnational, or indigenous concerns *and* simultaneously critiquing "imperialist strategies of representing, objectifying and exhibiting the Other" (Chow 1995:44).

Jhabvala's statement and Chow's "O" (perhaps the new "Oriental" or the victim complicit with her sadomasochistic lover in Réage's *The Story of O*) both point to liberal white academe's collusion in the process of "othering" and its self-serving agenda. The nexus of identity formation and representation in these two narratives is clearly the result, in many ways serendipitous, of three contemporary sociocultural phenomena:

1. the reality of educated classes in formerly colonized countries,

2. the new wave of immigration from Asia to the West, especially to the United States, and

3. the needs and fantasies of "activist" Western academics and university administrators concerned with the "bottom line."

We noted in the last chapter that the nature of educated Indian immigration and the responses of Indian high castes and nonminority Americans to affirmative action initiatives provide an essential element of this pandemic othering. In many ways, the immigration of intellectuals is a familiar occurrence. Certain consequences of the present immigration are, however, unprecedented. We must remember that the first large wave of Indians immigrated under the special skills provisions of the 1965 Immigration Act and that these provisions totally skewed the demographics of South Asian Americans. Unlike other immigrant populations, Indians who immigrated from the 1960s onward were exclusively professionals.[2] Between 1966 and 1977, 83 percent of the Indian immigrants were categorized as professional or technical workers, with twenty thousand scientists with PhDs, forty thousand engineers, and twenty-five thousand medical doctors (Prashad 2000:75). It was not only the skills of the South Asian intellectual population that were exceptional. They fit seamlessly into the contemporary academic milieu and served a specific political purpose.

We have also argued that administrators employ Asian "people of color" to fulfill minority hiring and diversity quotas. Moreover, given their class backgrounds, Indian immigrants tend to share the racial values and attitudes of middle- and upper-middle-class white Americans. Historically, Aryan Indians have always distinguished themselves from their Other in terms of their high spirituality and civilization (Figueira 2002). They exported this racial ideology to America as early as Vivekananda's tour in 1893. This self-image allows Indian Americans (Desis) to position themselves in such a way that they can believe themselves to be superior to American blacks, an attractive position for a migrant in search of some accommodation in a racist polity (Prashad 2000:xi). Moreover, there exists an unconscious or semiconscious need on the part of white academics to identify with and support the post-colonial intellectual. South Asians seem to satisfy their fantasies and longings for "revolution," "freedom," "the primitive," "cutting edge," and so on. The fulfillment of such exoticist fantasies may, indeed, provide the structuring force behind the entire enterprise of postcolonial criticism. In order to interrogate the psycho-political impulses motivating postcolonialism's projections onto a phantasmic Other, we may wish to extend our evaluation of postcolonial theory and analyze its development and methodological history.

POSTCOLONIAL CRITICISM'S DISCIPLINARY ROOTS

While postcolonial criticism traces its lineage to the critique of Orientalism initiated by Edward Said in the 1970s,[3] it can be analyzed further back to the anthropological model of area studies. It was in this form that the non-European world was first systematically studied and taught in the United States during the 1950s and 1960s. In North American research institutions, area studies developed as a repudiation of the mode of conceptualizing the East that Said would later define as Orientalism. Its formation had everything to do with the cold war and the demands of the national security state. Area studies originated out of armed service language schools. It initially focused on Japanese, Korean, Chinese, and Vietnamese language training but grew to include most other Asian languages. Such programs met a cold war need to communicate with potential enemies.

Area studies specialists worked in conjunction with indigenous scholars. The research of native scholars relied on the authority of their personal experience and was structured to mirror the structures of explanation valued in Western scientific discourse (Hancock 1998:357). As "culture brokers," native informants derived social and material privilege from their efforts. Area studies specialists then repackaged the native informant's experiential knowledge and disseminated it. Relying on the data provided by native informants, they created an objectifying discourse in which the site of a national culture was "imagined." In the case of India, these scholars documented and managed the internal Others (tribals, peasants, minority populations), whom the barely nascent Indian state sought to mold into a nation. Area studies specialists exercised hegemonic power by "privileging the contingent boundaries of the Indian state as natural delimiters of cultural forms" (Hancock 1998:347). The native informants served as disciplinary gatekeepers providing an authoritative version of Indian history (Hancock 1998:344) for upper-caste Indians (reformers or nationalists) and the West. In fact, by their methodological reliance on native informants and political use of their data to affix claims on the nation, area studies specialists did not differ essentially from the Orientalists who preceded them. Both provided a conceptualization of Asia underwritten by state and private capital.[4] Both produced their own brand of Orientalism.

Postcolonial criticism replicates the sites and subject positions traditionally apportioned to area studies to such a degree that Spivak has identified the objectified subject of the postcolonial Other with the native informant (Spivak 1986:235–39).[5] Postcolonial criticism encompasses what Rey Chow has distinguished as the four major types of analysis in cultural studies:

1. The critique of Orientalism and its racial hierarchizing developed by Said

2. The Subaltern critique of class and gender, promulgated by Spivak[6]

3. Minority discourse analysis influenced by Deleuze, Guattari, and Jan Mohammed

4. The notion of hybridity as championed by Bhabha. (Chow 2002: 105–06)[7]

The production of postcoloniality has played a central role in critics' attempts at self-fashioning. In fact, as a form of cultural studies, postcolonial criticism has come to perform a similar function with regard to Indian national identity narratives as Orientalist scholars and area studies specialists carried out in the past. Moreover, the focus of postcolonial criticism has shifted in the process of its institutionalization. Once commodified, postcolonial criticism has come to serve developmental needs within the university as well as identificatory structures both in academe and the diaspora community at large.

Cultural studies developed out of the reformulation of language, with the shift away from the structural linguistic approach to an emphasis on the relations between representation and politics.[8] In the wake of structuralism, literature, once a central mode of aesthetic expression, had come to be viewed as an anachronistic form of cultural capital. The paradigm shift from the literary to the cultural studies model presumably sought to install a more immediate and less conservative hierarchical format where cultural products of everyday life are valorized in protest of bourgeois elitism and the commodification of high art. Following the trend established by Barthes in *Mythologies*, cultural studies enables a range of populist production (advertising and popular genres such as thrillers, romances, film, music, and fashion) to be read like literary texts. It presents a cult of vernacular experience as a substitute for historical analysis (San Juan 2002:225).[9] In area studies, work had been undertaken in the name of scientific objectivity, knowledge acquisition, and cross-cultural understanding. Cultural studies pretends no such innocent motivation. It presupposes the existence of exploitation and asymmetrical power relations inherent in all Western studies of non-Western culture. The sites previously studied in area studies would become deconstructed in cultural studies as target fields.

Cultural studies came into being in the context of what has been termed the "victim revolution" on campuses (D'Souza 1991:191) and flourished in an era where concepts such as 'truth' were read to mean 'bias,' and 'knowledge' invariably was translated as ideology (Rapaport 2001:98). Lawrence Grossberg, a key theorist in the field, envisioned cultural studies as taking place simultaneously with political critique and intervention (Grossberg, Nelson, and Treichler 1992). This initial conceptualization proved to be the essential problem at the heart of cultural studies. If all popular practices are seen as positive resistance to domination, the very possibilities of any real revolutionary change are trivialized (San Juan 2002:228). There can be no empowering if "everyday tactical dissembling" becomes politically progressive. The very substitution of a populist program is itself a trivialization of subaltern actors and local knowledges (San Juan 2002:225). Cultural studies very quickly degenerated into an apology for commodity fetishism. Essentially, there was no need for social struggle if television and shopping malls were already "theaters of subversion" (Mulhern 1995:40; cited in San Juan 2002:227).

The shift from the aesthetic to the cultural studies model took place at roughly the same time that area studies had reached a crisis point due to the change in priorities occasioned by global capitalism. As any region's historical and geographic boundaries become contested, its political and strategic value also undergoes redefinition. When such changes occur, institutions need to justify maintaining programs and scholars that people them (Hancock 1998:373). Language programs, the former mainstay for graduate funding and faculty lines were downsized, absorbed into larger units, or even cut when they were no longer subsidized by Defense Department funding due to shifts in national priorities.[10] Such radical shifts in strategic significance and funding occurred in area studies at roughly the same time that Said specifically linked the development of colonial knowledge to the beginnings of Orientalist scholarship and suggested that its growth was tied to area studies,[11] a latter-day institutionalization of Orientalism.

It was a bad time for area studies specialists in general. Their legitimization and funding were waning at the very moment that their Orientalist legacy was being unmasked. Said's association of area studies with colonial knowledge (a linkage made as early as 1950 in Schwab's *La Renaissance orientale* for whose English translation Said wrote an introduction in 1984) should have signaled the occasion to rethink the practice of area studies, put it on a less politically mediated basis of knowledge, and free it from its reliance on the cold war necessities of the national security state. This task, however, was never taken up by area studies specialists. It was not the moment to rise to the challenge posed by *Orientalism* and reassess their disciplinary practices. The stakes were just too high. It would have entailed area studies programs acknowledging and coming to terms with their reliance on the necessities of the national security state. Perhaps the challenge was not accepted because instrumentality had been implanted in such programs *ab initio* (Harootunian 2002:152–53). Or perhaps area studies did not question its Orientalist roots because its practitioners, a group of liberal-thinking professors, might have had to question the neocolonialist origins of their jobs or the neocolonialist character of their research, faculty recruitment, and funding. It is hard to be alternative or radical when the State Department has funded your entire career and continues to cut your checks.

Area studies programs, however, did realize that they needed to change. The places, people, and pasts to be studied needed to be reconceptualized out of an urgency to acknowledge new postsubjectivities. In response, universities created new models to satisfy changing priorities. They produced new visions of international studies that promised new knowledge required for participation in new globalizing systems of production and consumption. Such new transnational "ethnoscapes" supplanted the threatened traditional area studies departments.

Although the critique initiated by Said did not engender any fundamental soul searching in social science methodology beyond the cosmetic,[12] it did find fertile ground in the humanities, especially English studies. A site such as India, formerly housed in religion, anthropology, linguistics, and area studies conglomerates, would now, thanks to the critique of Orientalism, find a home and theoretical resources in English departments, ethnic studies, women's studies, humanities centers, and cultural studies units (Hancock 1998:374). An important thing to note about these locales is that they did not necessarily demand any site-specific knowledge of languages or historical context. "Doing" India in such a setting often means that one does not need to learn specifics about India at all.

India could emigrate to an English department because, for the greater part of the 1980s and 1990s, English literature departments on many campuses had waged successful battles with other administrative units, especially comparative literature, to become the campus experts on theory. Since comparative and national literature scholars had translated and written primers for recent European theory, all English departments now had to do was step in and anoint themselves the true scholars of critical thought and commandeer the enrollments that went along with the theory craze. On many campuses, this turf war was brutal, since comparative literature departments did not have the critical mass to fight the hegemonic onslaughts of huge English departments.[13] With the appropriation of theory, numerous English departments chose to supplement their curricula with courses dealing less with literature per se and more with issues of identity and its construction (Harootunian 2002:152–53). As theory emigrated to English, so too did all those subfields dealing with identity politics, such as feminist, psychoanalytic, and postcolonial studies. The task of rethinking the mission of regions outside Europe (the third world) was thus coopted by English departments and humanities centers (Harootunian 2002:167). We should not lose sight of the fact that this appropriation by English studies of "identity" studies opened the field of possible specializations within a discipline that found it increasingly difficult to place the PhDs it had been producing within the more traditional paradigms of English literature. Identity studies such as postcolonial criticism and multiculturalism were boons to English departments. They not only offered English departments a politically correct identity but also provided additional marketable subfields of critical knowledge. In fact, they provided a new field entirely and countless possible openings for any number of job and degree candidates. It is not, therefore, by chance that English studies incorporated identity studies precisely at the time when its graduate programs were overpopulated with students with diminishing prospects and few viable subjects left for dissertations and few jobs available in canonical fields and authors.[14] Some English studies programs acquired tropes and subjects from any number of disciplines, and in the new possible combinations, new dissertation topics opened up new positions. New subfields, such as ethnicity studies, multiculturalism, transnationalism, diasporic studies, and postcolonial studies, sprang up, purporting to cross spatial as well as disciplinary borders.

Just as area studies had earlier privileged a given region, postcolonial criticism now valorized the formation of subjectivity and a politics of identity rooted in location. In both area studies and postcolonial criticism, the locations under investigation (the Middle East or South Asia) were often not even real entities but rather geographical imaginary zones existing only in government bureaus and academic institutions. Just as English departments had become the spokespersons of theory and ethnicity, so too they now became the custodians of the world, developing an institution's administrative units on alterity. Theory and the world, once the purview of comparative literature departments, were now taught in English departments, often without historical contextualization or any grasp of the source texts. In fact, English departments were reinventing the wheel. They were uninformed or willfully ignorant of the fact that comparative literature programs had for decades been doing the very type of work that they now envisioned as cutting edge. In their provincialism, worldly English scholars could now claim: "In a globalized world, it is perhaps time to think in terms of comparative and transnational multiculturalism, of relational studies that do not always pass through the putative order. What are the relationalities between Indian and Egyptian cinema?" (Shohat and Stam 2003:4). One can only question whether English professors had ever previously pondered what their colleagues in comparative literature had been doing for the last thirty years. Those English departments, now bemoaning Eurocentrism, were unaware that comparatists had engaged in such cross-cultural analyses for decades. A generation ago René Etiemble advised Western comparatists to be conversant in at least one non-Western language and literature. English departments were now congratulating themselves for suggesting the type of inquiry that comparative literature had been doing for years without subtitles!

The practicality of English departments' incorporation of ethnicity and postcolonial studies was that they could in many institutions colonize the now discredited area studies programs and the smaller (and, therefore) vulnerable comparative literature programs. By reading the world in translation, English departments uncovered racist oppression and, at the same time, waged an effective imperialistic campaign of their own. In fact, one might argue that postcolonial criticism gave English departments a new lease on life and the politically expedient cause of officially combating imperialist mentalities of the past while waging a disciplinary hegemonic offensive in the present.

The monopolization of postcolonial studies by English studies effected an important change in focus. Postcolonial studies, of necessity, became more textual, semiotic, and general. Had postcolonial studies stayed in the field of area studies, it would have emphasized social sciences and political economy, as in the model of the Delhi-based Subaltern Studies Group (Harootunian 2002:168). Once postcolonial criticism had migrated to English, however, it lost any interest in history it might have had, jettisoning an already modest association with such things as temporality and chronologies. By appealing to culturalism as a putative structuring force, postcolonial criticism led to a supersession of history and an articulation of formalist exceptionalism where history seems to have been completed in archaic times (Harootunian 2002:153). As one critic has opined, postcolonial criticism became (in much the same way as multiculturalism had) an overblown, overdetermined, and amorphous discourse repudiating any meaningful specificity of historical location or interpretation (Krishnaswamy 1995:128).

In the migration of India as a disciplinary site to the field of English studies, we find a situation akin to that described by Arjun Appadurai as the aesthetics of decontextualization, where ethnic products become authentic through cultural dislocation. Appadurai cites the study of third-world literature in English departments as a case in point (Appadurai 1986:28). Through a process wherein readers sympathetically identify with such decontextualized products, cultural ignorance not only results but is also sanctioned. Postcolonial criticism allowed us to accept a politics of ignorance and the perpetuation of ignorance-as-knowledge, especially in our classrooms (Srivastava 1995:16). This state of affairs describes how India often gets "taught" in the States today.[15]

COMMODIFYING POSTCOLONIAL THEORY AND TYPE-CASTING THE CRITIC

Postcolonial theory provides a test case for Guillory's critique of the institutional leveling out of putatively marginal cultural forms (Guillory 1993:37–38). Disparate postcolonial texts, collectively studied in English and coopted for a largely imaginary pedagogic agenda, are deployed as forms of cultural capital in an institutional setting. With postcolonial literature thus grounded, it becomes an oppositional academic discipline as well as an attractive and nonthreatening object of consumption.

On the institutional level, postcolonial theory has become a fetishized commodity (Ahmad 1992:127). This process involves turning the literatures and cultures of the non-West into saleable exotic objects, such as multicultural anthologies and highly publicized first novels by young authors who are *de facto* spokespersons for their place of birth (Brennan 1997:47–48). The fight for spokespersonship can get nasty. Who speaks for the voiceless oppressed Other? The "native" whose education and life experience bespeaks privilege or liberal self-minoritized whites who have studied under them? The cosmopolitan alterity industry perfected a rhetoric of fetishized otherness (Huggan 2001:10), where sympathetic identification masks the transformation of power politics into spectacle (Arac and Ritvo 1991:3). These very gestural and performative aspects, in fact, make them suspect. They offer too convenient a structure for career development (Krishnaswamy 1995:128).

Commodifying the third world serves concrete development needs. Universities have suffered some downsizing in recent years. With the loss of public funding, state and private institutions have had to target special interest groups in order to fund new initiatives. Diasporic groups have become increasingly instrumental in such development projects. Indian Americans, who comprise the richest immigrant demographic group in the United States, present tremendous economic potential as evidenced by recent Indian-based endowments of chairs in major public and private universities. Institutions have become quite adept at catering (some might say, pandering) to such groups.

If vested interest groups fund a program, one can be sure that an "official," that is, politically acceptable, representation of that nation, its people, and its cultural products is promoted. Appeals to cultural nationalism are implicit in institutional development efforts (Grewal 1994). Moreover, since universities are recruiting Indian American students in ever-increasing numbers, it is only logical that they would solicit courses focusing on their communities and concerns. Ideally, these courses would be user-friendly, not challenging religious or communalist sympathies. Once again, courses that focus on the victimization of a people under colonial rule do not threaten a diaspora community's idealized view of the homeland. Postcolonial theoretical initiatives can thus dovetail very nicely with marketing concerns.

Vijay Prashad has attributed the rise and power of diaspora groups to the manner in which Indian Americans have sought to maintain and transmit their culture in isolation through cultural organizations (based on Indian languages and regions) that choose to define culture in religious terms in order to present themselves to the white power structure as a cultural commodity (Prashad 2000:142–43). Diasporic "cultural" groups maintain strong ties to Indian political parties, especially the major vehicles of the Hindu Right, such as the Vishwa Hindu Parishad (VHP) and the Bharatiya Janata Party (BJP). These parties came to prominence in the 1980s, pushing a Hindutva (Syndicated Brahmanical Hinduism) platform with two major issues: destroying the sixteenth-century mosque built on what was thought to be the site of the Hindu god Rama's birthplace (symbolically ending the habit of "coddling" Muslim sensibilities) and the end of compensatory positive discrimination to oppressed castes (a dispute over the report of the Mandal Commission upholding affirmative action). The VHP has brilliantly exploited the resources available from nonresident Indians in the West (NRIs). Playing upon immigrant guilt, the Hindu Right has funded their initiatives through allied cultural associations such as the Vishwa Hindu Parishad of America (VHPA). The VHPA acts through its student wing, the Hindu Students Council (HSC), which champions Hindutva as the neglected culture of Hindu Americans. The HSC has moved away from the sectarian violence promulgated in India by the BJP; VHP; their ideological precursor, the Rashtriya Swayamsevak Sangh (RSS); and gang Hindu activists of the Bajrang Pal. It has consciously entered "into the multicultural space opened up in the liberal academy" where it can promote what some consider the "neglected virtues of an ancient civilization" (Prashad 2000:144). Claiming merely to be cultural organizations, the VHPA and the HSC can thus officially distance themselves from the very political groups of which they are offshoots.

The Hindutva elements in the diaspora community have been more vocal and active in their involvement in scholarly matters. Much recent funding of Indian studies in the United States has come from groups with Hindu nationalist ties and fundamentalist sympathies. Allegiances to such groups have dictated how India, and particularly its religion, are taught. A prime example of this trend can be seen in the Hinduja family's sponsorship of a Vedic studies center at Columbia University. There has also been a considerably orchestrated movement within the diaspora community to control how Indian religion is emplotted within Western scholarship. In particular, Wendy Doniger, the Mircea Eliade Professor of History of Religions at the University of Chicago, has come under intense fire, as have those deemed her "children," for having distorted Hinduism (Braverman 2004:32–35; Rothstein 2005).

Unlike the native informant of the area studies model, the native specialist in today's "marketing of India" is positioned in the forefront, producing and not just authenticating the discourse on national identity. Trained in Western critical epistemes, indigenous scholars based in the West can provide a discourse on national culture that purports to challenge racialized, gendered, and class inequalities written into the structures of knowledge. Unfortunately, the possibility that these visions might just "play back into exclusionary nationalisms" (Hancock 1998:375) is not questioned. It is ironic that the colonized elite, whose victimization is mourned, but whose collaborative role in colonialism and neocolonialism is never problematized, are the ancestors and brethren of the immigrant population that shoulders the largest tax burden in the United States. We have now arrived at a stage in the emplotment of India where the Orientalist and area studies models have been replaced by what might be termed the "immigrant imaginary" (Rafael 1994:104) or where teaching becomes an autoethnographic exercise (Brennan 1997:115). It is this "immigrant imaginary" that fuels postcolonial criticism, finances an idealized portrayal of a wealthy and powerful ethnic community, and determines the role that the critic warmly embraces.

As we have noted, identity studies, among which we place postcolonial criticism, do not tend to question how well the construction of the text as a network of hegemonic or subversive gestures suits the state of literary theoretical professionalization. Moreover, it does not examine the manner in which the critic's self-fashioning through imaginary marginalization results primarily in the wide-ranging identification of an academic privileged class with the marginalized Other. The historically oppressed have become the new role models for the critic, giving political authority to the search for cultural difference. In a quasimessianic manner, the postcolonial critic positions him- or herself to speak for the oftimes neocolonized Other. The critic can claim to talk for the margin and, in doing so, also pretend to speak from the margin, while actually inhabiting a space that is quite close to the center.

Homi Bhabha's earnest attempt to recast theory as a "politics of the theoretical statement" (1989:114) exemplifies this casting of the critic as a fellow traveler alongside the disenfranchised, as he argues for a reconsideration of Lenin's famous question in poststructuralist terms:

> "What is to be done?" must acknowledge the force of writing, its meta-phoricity and its rhetorical discourse, as a productive matrix, which defines the "social" and makes it available as an objective of and for, action. Textu-ality is not simply a second-order ideological subject. . . . A knowledge can only become political through an agnostic process: dissensus, alterity and otherness are the discursive conditions for the circulation and recognition of a politicized subject and a public "truth." (Bhabha 1989:115)

This passage from Bhabha's oft-cited essay "The Commitment to Theory" is symptomatic of the problem I have been outlining in at least two ways. First, the critic's placement of "social" and "truth" within quotation marks effectively reduces the real world struggles of the disenfranchised to a dis-cursive problem. In his deft deconstruction of a politics/theory opposition that would privilege praxis, the critic necessarily ends up valorizing what he does—write, theorize—without requiring any further commitment from him. Theory is a form of praxis, Bhabha wants to argue—I am already doing my bit. This line of argumentation leads to the conclusion—my second point—that the critic is in fact already aligned with the disenfranchised. Through his claim of the solidarity of theory with the politics of change, Bhabha can implicitly align himself with the disenfranchised or at least what he terms in the essay's conclusion a "free people of the future" (Bhabha 1989:131), even as the actual struggles of people all but disappear in his analysis. In one of its most disturbing moments, the essay in fact reduces these individuals to discursive figures:

> [Theory] makes us aware that our political referents and priorities—the people, the community, class, struggle, antiracism, gender difference, the assertion of an anti-imperialist, black or third perspective—are not there in some primordial, naturalistic sense. Nor do they reflect a unitary or homogeneous object. *They make sense as they come to be constructed* in the discourses of feminism or Marxism or the Third Cinema or whatever, whose objects of priority—class or sexuality or "the new ethnicity"—are always in historical or philosophical tension, or cross-reference with other objectives. (Bhabha 1989:118, emphasis added)

Here, the critic's self-aggrandizing agenda and role-playing become crystal clear. Theory is not only an indispensable part of the struggle, Bhabha claims: I produce the struggle and along with it the very people with whom it simultaneously (and cynically) claims solidarity. Thus Bhabha's "Commitment to Theory" allows the critic to have it both ways: it would preempt any critique of how the text's appearance as a network of hegemonic or subversive gestures undermines the political causes it claims to champion in favor of literary professionalism, while allowing the critic, simultaneously, to pose as a champion of the people "committed to progressive political change in the direction of a socialist society" (Bhabha 1989:113). Any question of real powerlessness or marginalization—such as that of the efficacy of theory to effect change—disappears, to be replaced by a posture of powerlessness steeped in a discourse of hybridity, indeterminacy of the signifier, and so on. Theory thus validates the theorist's social pose, even as it absolves him of making any real difference. It is significant that by 2003, Bhabha can reject the uncritical valorization of the nomad figure and insist that "immigrants . . . and nomads don't merely circulate. They need to settle, claim asylum or nationality, demand housing . . . assert their economic and cultural rights and come to be legally represented" (Bhabha 2003:237). Yet his prescription for addressing intolerable conditions trails off into the familiar vagaries of theoretical discourse: "For such rights and equalities to exist . . . we must possess the cautious virtue of political tolerance, but we must go beyond it to cultivate the virtuosity of cultural *poésis* that allows us to speak of the world as we make it in tongues that are not our own" (Bhabha 2003:237).

This masquerade poses a significant problem of representation. By drawing on the experiences of displacement and desire for home as part of the diasporic experience, postcolonial criticism uses these experiences to deconstruct a deterritorialized identity politics. Postcolonial texts abound with examples of this kind of theoretical legerdemain and its corresponding dearth of cultural specificity: Said's sweeping indictment of the entire Western civilization in *Orientalism*; Bhabha's dizzying (and never fully worked through) invocation of Salman Rushdie, Franz Fanon, Goethe, two Latino performance artists,[16] and Toni Morrison's *Beloved* in the introduction to *The Location of Culture*; and Spivak's facile juxtaposition of W. E. B. Du Bois and José Martí in the long parenthesis that concludes *Death of a Discipline* (2003).[17]

Postcolonial criticism must reflect postmodernism's concern with hybridity and sites of ambivalence because theoretical notions of the margin, periphery, and exilic space allow critics to create a metaphorical space in which to dwell that is separate from the real space they inhabit. In this metaphorical space, critics can voice ideologies of subversion and rebellion that would be too unsettling, if voiced from their own actual space. Critics' delicate balancing acts stem from the paradox of inhabiting a space of bourgeois comfort, while at the same time needing to distance themselves from global capitalism. When critics appropriate the metaphorical space of the postcolonial, nomad, exile, and marginal, they hope to exonerate themselves for all the benefits they receive from this same capitalism. Criticism thus functions as an act of penance, or, to give it a clinical diagnosis, criticism becomes an expression of false consciousness: the reified perception made up of identificatory, antidialectical, and egocentric structures that existential psychoanalysis exposed more than thirty years ago.

FALSE CONSCIOUSNESS

In a seminal work in the field of social psychology, Joseph Gabel defined false consciousness as a dissociation produced by a reification of the past (Gabel 1975:253ff). False consciousness is primarily a distortion of the perception and experience of time. When the natural flow of time is "dissociated" by ideology, utopianism, or schizophrenia, it produces a perception that is out of touch with reality and at odds with historical fact; it becomes false consciousness (Gabel 1975:xiv). Existential psychoanalysis views the constructions of reality by ideologues, schizophrenics, and utopian idealists as similar. They are all seen to seek reification of their historical existence and understanding of their visions as an organized system of meaning produced to balance and disguise the disorder of their being-in-the-world (Gabel 1975:22). In postcolonial criticism, an analogous process is at work. The emphasis on the Self overshadows the testimony of native voices.

Homi Bhabha's invocation of both *Beloved* and the plight of border-crossing Mexican immigrants in the introduction to *The Location of Culture,* for example, functions in precisely this way, by invoking the struggles of African American slaves and Latino communities only as a point of departure for his own discursive analysis of hybridity and the transposibility of cultural positions (Bhabha 1994:6–18). Bhabha's by-now-notorious refrain, "Who is Beloved?" (1994:18) emerges in this context as disingenuous and even cynical, given that the novel's very obvious positioning of Beloved herself—arguably among the most poignant characters in all of American literature—is reduced in Bhabha's analysis to a rhetorical figure in a broader analysis that ultimately confirms the critic's place as an arbiter of culture and spokesman for the Other.

Spivak's translations of Mahasweta Devi's fiction and her writing on the practice of sati in India, while more subtle and self-reflexive in their maneuverings, function in much the same way. Spivak is less interested in the stories themselves, which focus on the plight of the *devadasis*, than on how they serve as examples of her own theory of subalternity, as best explained in her well-known essay "Can the Subaltern Speak?" (1988a). Spivak downplays the horrors perpetrated upon the protagonist of Devi's "Breast-Giver," for example, in favor of the broader argument about the incommensurability of subalternity and representation (Spivak 1988b:222–68). Likewise, Spivak's discussions of the case of the widowed Rani of Sirmur and the politically motivated suicide of a young militant Indian woman finally shift away from the individuals' respective predicaments and toward presenting them as examples of an "unemphatic, ad hoc, subaltern rewriting of the social text of *sati*-suicide" (Spivak 1999:307). Spivak goes on to further contextualize the women's struggles within an abstracted theoretical framework, concluding ambivalently that "[t]he subaltern as female, cannot be heard or read. . . . Bhubaneswari attempted to 'speak' by turning her body into a text of woman/writing" and that "her attempt had failed" because later generations of women in her own family failed to "hear" her correctly (Spivak 1999:308). In each of these examples, the native voice of the subaltern is sublated and folded into the critic's larger theoretical imperatives, first among which is the self-positioning in an imaginary solidarity with the marginalized Other who cannot speak. The native voice becomes mere fodder for the critic's performance of a virtuous marginality. Absent, of course, from this discussion is the fact that any archival investigations of native and colonial records show ample evidence of subaltern women "speaking" for themselves (Waters 1997).

The problem with this postcolonial formulation becomes clear, as San Juan suggests, "when contraposed to the resistance of colonized subalterns themselves" (San Juan 1998:8). The truly marginalized are not there by choice; they do not, as does the postcolonial critic, position themselves on the perceived margin the better to produce elaborate academic critiques of Western hegemony. If for Bhabha, Said, and others the margin is a desirable place from which to exploit the "unevenness" of colonial discourses, for Arif Dirlik such a posture of self-marginalization emphasizes cultural difference and linguistic indeterminacy (the critic's strengths) at the expense of a more substantial critique of Western hegemony: "However much postcolonial intellectuals may insist on hybridity and the transposability of locations, not all positions are equal in power, as Spivak's interrogators in India seem to recognize in their reference to the 'wings of progress' that brought her to India. To insist on hybridity against one's own language, it seems to me, is to disguise not only ideological location but also the differences of power that go with different locations" (Dirlik 1994:343). Dirlik's critique, like San Juan's, effectively gives the lie to postcolonial formulations of Foucault's theory of marginality by exposing the irreducible difference between the critic and the subaltern group. Critics may conspicuously position themselves at the margin, but they retain a mobility (social and literal) that the truly disenfranchised can only dream of. As Michael Gorra points out in a different context, the fluidity and hybridity that postcolonialism so prizes "remain[s] best suited for those most able to live with a sense of uncertainty and improvisation—for the gifted and well-off, those for whom shuttling between London and Bombay is the literal and not the figurative truth" (Gorra 1997:172).[18]

What I propose instead is that we reject a postcolonial theory that, as practiced by its most eminent stars, glorifies legerdemain and linguistic pyrotechnics at the expense of the careful study of languages, literatures, and cultures—precisely those skills and habits that, ironically enough, Spivak herself praises throughout her recent work as the traditional strengths of comparative literature. If the rise of postcolonial studies poses any real threat to comparative literature as a discipline, it is because of the apparent ease with which an initiate can become an expert. Because postcolonial theory does not require comparative literature's linguistic skills nor an expert's familiarity with specific national cultures and histories, it allows for (and even encourages) a theoretical approach that conflates individual colonial histories and contexts into an overarching "condition." Thus postcolonialism's false consciousness: postcolonial studies emerges as a faux discipline whose practitioners can celebrate cultural difference and hybridity and speak in solidarity with subalterns without ever having to partake of their actual struggles. They can gain a marketable specialization without too much effort or need for theoretical, political, and cultural homework (Srivastava 1995:15).

What born-again comparatist Spivak calls for in *The Death of a Discipline*—a "reconstellation" of the discipline that retains its traditional strengths while embracing a suspiciously postcolonial-sounding "planetarity" (Spivak 2003:91)—again promises to do everything in the manner of a demonstrably overinflated postcoloniality: preserve traditional strengths while opening up to cultural and linguistic differences within national literatures and retain and defend the value of language skills. True to the postcolonial approach I have mapped out, Spivak asserts all this but offers only an anecdotal, willfully eclectic exposition of what such a comparative literature might look like, how it might operate in a world increasingly dominated by facile monolingual postcolonial and cultural studies. Rather than a prescription or manifesto, Spivak presents the book as a call to action "in the hope that there may be some in the academy who do not believe that the critical edge of the humanities should be appropriated and determined by the market" (Spivak 2003:xii). This approach is, of course, consistent with the postcolonial critic's pretense of "openness" toward the future as Spivak herself asserts that "we must, as literature teachers in the classroom . . . let literature teach us that there are no certainties, that the process is open, and that it may be salubrious that it is so" (Spivak 2003:26).

Perhaps. But then again, *plus ça change, plus c'est la même chose.* Spivak's strategy exemplifies the dishonesty pervading much postcolonial theory. It espouses an open-endedness in order to occlude a concerted lack of cultural knowledge, specificity, and ultimately, respect for the cultures supposedly being studied. Such lofty disinterest allows Spivak in a final, unfortunate parenthesis at the end of *Death of a Discipline* to blithely throw together figures as disparate as José Martí and W. E. B. Du Bois for no better reason than that they represent "two widely known, heroic figures from the older minorities, writers of a previous dispensation" (Spivak 2003:92). She can invoke the two great modernists not to carefully discuss their works but to employ them in her own critical project of "the turning of identitarian monuments into documents for reconstellation" (Spivak 2003:91). It is a profoundly disappointing yet not surprising conclusion for the book. It points in a discouraging way to how one of our discipline's most renowned professors practices her craft. Martí and Du Bois do not need to be "reconstellated," but Spivak's version of comparative literature does.

Postcolonial criticism has, in fact, died. It died before we could even articulate adequately what it was. It is time for critics to retool themselves. What better persona to adopt, in the age of multiculturalism and globalism, than that of a comparatist? Postcolonial critics, whose formation had been almost exclusively in English literature, made their careers championing a brand of criticism that claimed to engage a voiceless, underrepresented world. They did so while ignoring the methodology and linguistic expertise traditional to the discipline of comparative literature. They now position themselves as prophets calling for a return to the very skills that their own scholarship has consistently eschewed. They claim to engage in a reform process of installing the standards of cultural and linguistic specificity to a discipline that their own brand of criticism had coopted and colonized.[19] They claim to discover what comparatists have known and practiced for decades, with the telling difference that the focus continues to be on the consciousness of the critic herself rather than the culture supposedly under investigation. This too is an extension of the false consciousness that plagues scholars today.

COMMODITY FETISHISM AND BRAHMINIZATION

The institutionalization of postcolonialism described above exhibits a process of commodity fetishism or the veiling of the material circumstances under which a commodity is produced and consumed. Commodity fetishism has three components. It involves a mystification or leveling out of historical experience. It also exhibits an imagined access to the cultural Other and entails the reification of people and places into aesthetic objects. Postcolonial criticism fits these criteria. It presents the historical past often more informed by ideology than by historical and linguistic facts. This distorted vision of the past, dissociated from reality, is further circumscribed by the critic's strategies of self-representation. By reifying the history of colonialism, making it the sole source of all sociocultural evils, postcolonial critics foreclose the possibility of interrogating and transcending the endemic social and cultural dysfunction that predates colonialism and lives on after the colonial masters have left. In this respect, postcolonial critics not only exhibit a false consciousness. Through a process of brahminization, literary critics reify their own position within both their professional and ethnic communities.[20]

The term *brahminization* was first introduced by anthropologist M. N. Srinivas in the 1950s to describe the process, also known as "Sanskritization,"[21] whereby a group attempts to acquire the traditional symbols of high status (customs, rituals, and lifestyle) of the local highest elite (Srinivas 1966:28).[22] 'Brahminization' denotes the social and ritual emulation of brahmins (Srinivas 1956:482–84). In Hindu society, brahmins are the original culture brokers who control scripture and materially profit from its manipulation and dissemination.[23] 'Brahminization' well suits our argument, since brahmins, as traditional interpreters of Hindu scriptures, are the archetypal ideal readers and authoritative critics (Figueira 2002). Postcolonial critics, who appropriate the voice of the colonized subject and become professional spokespersons for alterity, in effect "brahminize" themselves, since they claim the power to disseminate images of the national culture and its internal Others, documenting and managing the Other through an objectifying discourse. This process essentially denotes the hermeneutical task of the brahmin with regard to scripture.[24]

Like the native informant of anthropology, postcolonial critics use their own experience to package a structure concerning India that reflects values and intellectual paradigms esteemed in the West. In this effort, they exercise power by delimiting a vision of the nation that suits ideological and political concerns of the diaspora community. They see themselves as both creators and products of national identity. They become, in effect, as much culture brokers as any Orientalist or area studies specialist of the third world. Rather than serving colonial projects or Indian nationalist or cold war liberal agendas, they act as gatekeepers of an Indian immigrant imaginary. Like the anthropologist, they serve the interests of upper-caste Indians and offer authoritative versions of history that reflect the politics of their time. Postcolonial critics thus serve a constituency within the diaspora community that funds their jobs in the West as well as nationalist and fundamentalist projects in India. By emulating the values and prerogatives of the Western academic secular elite, indigenous postcolonial critics construct a product to be consumed by the West for bureaucratic ends and global marketing needs. Mimicry, posing as a sly form of resistance, is actually less a marker of colonial servility and more a nostalgic yearning for the reestablishment of caste order.

Postcolonial critics establish a pedagogy based on the moral presumption of the individual teacher as the self-appointed custodian and transmitter of a text's allegedly oppositional values. Such teachers arrogate a "brahminical" authority that derives from their experience of these cultures. This authority reconfirms the otherness of the place from which they and the texts they study are perceived to spring (Huggan 2001:246). The problem with such authority is as follows: students do not question it any more than believers question their priests. Theory should open up texts to interpretation, not seal them up as if they were holy writ.

Throughout this volume, I have given prominence to the Indological vector of the theoretical and disciplinary problems that I have addressed in this chapter. It has not been my intention to impose a parochial cast upon the relevant phenomena exposed in this investigation. It is just that the Indian conceptions of postcolonialism happen to predominate for the historical, economic, and social reasons that I have outlined. There are, certainly, plenty of other third-world academics and their first-world avatars, mimics, and pretenders whose concepts of identity, of multiculturalism, and of their scholarly roles approximate the brahminical paradigm. Indian theorists have made their stream of the *Tendenz* so apparent that it makes them conspicuous. Other nativist shamans from Latin America, the Caribbean, and Africa are simply eclipsed.

CHAPTER 5

THE ROMANCE OF EXILE

INTRODUCTION

As we have seen, a paradigm shift from the aesthetic to the political has occurred in the last two decades. One could reject the canon of dead white males in favor of the cultural studies and multicultural models. We have suggested that dismantling the canon often had less to do with installing a more immediate and less conservative hierarchical format and more to do with installing a new tribal authority. In order to pursue this line of inquiry further, we may want to examine postcolonialism's rhetoric of migrancy in light of the material conditions and ideological contexts of its cultural production, marketing, and consumption. The role that the cosmopolitan third-world intellectual plays in the manufacture of diasporic consciousness (Krishnaswamy 1995:127) also needs to be analyzed. The kind of intellectual and scholar that these theories and pedagogies have brought into prominence and their project of self-fashioning are of crucial importance. These new authorities are as entitled as those who have been rejected, perhaps more so, since their value is grounded in imaginative projections of the Self into another existence that is more effective than their own. The new authorities seek validation by identifying with victims of repression. The human need to exoticize (or aestheticize) individual experience can be poignant, except when it becomes a marketing strategy. The commodity that is being marketed is the third world. As we have seen, in many American universities the third world is packaged under the rubric of postcolonial literatures, and these are marketed through multiculturalism. With multiculturalism and postcolonialism, the Other has gained a status as a hypercommodity and is marketed as such (Huggan 2000:19).

Multiculturalism and postcolonialism have borrowed from postmodernism its vision of the fragmented and disconnected Self and have created a new type of intellectual, defined as someone who has dispensed with territorial affiliation and travels unencumbered through the world bearing the burden of a unique, yet representative, sensibility that refracts a fragmented and contingent condition (Krishnaswamy 1995:125). One figure has become a central trope in this critical discourse, appearing with some regularity and referred to interchangeably as "the exile" or "the nomad." Since this figure has little resonance outside the first world, we should probably question why the public persona of the postcolonial writer and critic assumes the role of autonomous and exuberant exile and why it is presented as uniquely equipped to mediate third-world realities to first-world needs. This figure also raises questions regarding the postcolonial condition, the role of gender, and the function of the diaspora community within the university. The exile/nomad functions as a "postmodern avatar of the free-floating bourgeois subject" and is presented often as the only true site of resistance (Krishnaswamy 1995:143). In this chapter, we will examine the extent to which metaphors of migrancy abound in recent literary criticism. We will also investigate why they have become meaningful and what issues are raised by their use. We have to think carefully about employing a vocabulary that appears liberatory to many but not to all. Images of flight can misleadingly suggest a notion of universal and equal mobility where none, in fact, exists.

SPOKESPERSONSHIP

Since the 1960s, contiguous with the final stages of decolonization, there was a sustained and significant uprooting of third-world peoples. The rhetoric of migrancy in contemporary theory, however, does not focus on tangible issues occurring in these locales in the years following the demise of colonialism. Very little attention is paid to the economic and political reasons motivating immigration. Rather, colonial discourse analysis has been primarily interested in postmodernist concerns with hybridized and syncretic views of the modern world. Postcolonialism's repudiations of fixity, for example, are not studied as political strategies of subversion within historical contexts but rather have been bracketed as playful postmodern rejections of transcendent unities (Krishnaswamy 1995:140).

In the work of Baudrillard, travel is presented as a spectacular form of amnesia where everything is to be discovered and then erased (Baudrillard 1986:25). Baudrillard posits the postmodern *bricoleur* as always in the process of fashioning his various locales, with locale seen as the lived contradictions of place and event (Probyn 1990:182–83). His theory of travel—where any part of the world can be recreated or made to stand for another—partially explains the widespread acceptance of the metaphor of the exile/nomad in recent theory. In a world of third-order simulacra, the encroaching pseudoplaces merge to eliminate geographical space entirely. This merger is a founding event; once it has taken place, the true (like the real) begins to be reproduced in the image of the pseudo, which then becomes the true (Morris 1988:5; cited in Probyn 1990:183). The merger of the imaginary and the real is of crucial importance for metaphorical identities to be seen as viable. It allows individuals to speak on behalf of others.

"Speaking for" someone, however, poses significant problems of representation. In structuralist terms, anyone who claims to represent another's needs, goals, or situation participates in the construction of another's subject position (Alcoff 1991–92:9). Such representations are not based on acts of discovery but are always mediated. As products of interpretation, they are by nature political, and their epistemic grounds of legitimacy are open to question. Feminists, in particular, have problematized the act of speaking for others and labeled it "arrogant," "unethical," and "politically illegitimate" (Kamuf 1997:121). Since their inception, African American and women's studies programs have flourished on the belief that advocacy for the oppressed should principally be done by the oppressed themselves, the underlying premise being the recognition of divergences in social location (Alcoff 1991–92:6–7). The practice of privileged people speaking for or on the behalf of less privileged persons was seen as having the possible result of reinforcing the oppression of the less privileged. Whereas in some areas (and here again, I choose the model of African American and women's studies), speaking on behalf of an oppressed population came in for considerable criticism, the same did not occur in the field of postcolonialism. Quite the contrary. It is, in fact, remarkable how the examination of the literary and cultural construction of negritude, a matter of colossal importance for American history, has had so little impact on the methodology of cultural studies, while the effects on excolonials of the public school prejudices of British soldiers/bureaucrats shape how we ought to read not only Faulkner but even Euripides. Postcolonial criticism is simply an elite metropolitan discourse that claims to speak for the voiceless postcolonial subject. Gayatri Spivak legitimized the process of "speaking back" for oppressed third-world subjects in her groundbreaking article "Can the Subaltern Speak?" (1988a).

Foucault and Deleuze refused to speak for others on the grounds that the oppressed can transparently represent their own true interests. Spivak, however, rejected the self-abnegating intellectual poses of Foucault and Deleuze, claiming that their position served only to conceal the actual authorizing power of retreating intellectuals who in their very retreat help to consolidate a particular conception of experience as transparent and self-knowing. In other words, using the techniques of deconstruction, Spivak justified, legitimized, and sanctified her claim to spokespersonship for the presumably voiceless subaltern. To mitigate what might appear to some as a usurpation of power, she repudiated the hidden hegemonic force of doing otherwise. As an alternative, Spivak even claimed to promote "listening to" as opposed to "speaking for." So we are to understand that she is not actually a spokesperson for the oppressed but rather their ideal good listener, who happens to publish her interpretation of their *Dasein*. "Listening to" as opposed to "speaking for" allows her to essentialize the oppressed as nonideologically constructed subjects. She can then claim to actually prefer the act of "speaking to," where the intellectual neither abnegates her role nor presumes an authenticity as oppressed but still allows for the possibility that the oppressed will produce a counter sentence that then suggests a new historical narrative (Alcoff 1991–92:22–23). However, it is still the critic's task to articulate, deconstruct, publish, and receive royalties and honors from such selfless acts of mediation. Spivak's jesuitical-brahmin logic notwithstanding, there is a serious problem in postcolonial criticism with authorization. As members of academe, we are authorized by our institutional positions to develop theories that express the ideas and needs of others (Alcoff 1991–92:7), but is it a valid practice in general to speak for others, even if we call it by another name?

But spokespersonship is not the only salient problem operant in the rhetoric of migrancy.[1] Exaggerated authority and its self-righteous assumption are only worth so much. To this heady brew is added a dose of victimhood "by proxy" (Bahri 1995:73). Postcolonialism, spawned as it is from ethnicity studies, taught critics that it was legitimate to assume the posture of minorities, even if their entire existence, both socially and economically, belied such a position. Innovative responses to affirmative action have made it possible for individuals to self-minoritize themselves. The heyday of being a minority might be over, if it ever really existed. There may even exist, in many circles, considerable backlash against minorities. Nevertheless, a new form of victimhood was useful, especially for those who could not feasibly claim minority status. Ideally, this identity would allow individuals to pose as victims without subjecting colleagues in the metropolitan milieu to any inconvenient or "unseemly minority behavior." Enter the exile, or rather, reenter the exile, since the exile already existed as a classic artistic persona.

THE EXILE

The embattled intellectual exile, sometimes called the "expatriate," was a major figure of modernism (Pound, Joyce, Conrad, Eliot). Aijaz Ahmad has attributed poststructural theories of migrancy to this literary tradition. Poststructuralism borrowed from modernism the representation of exile as a painful yet ennobling experience for artistic consciousness (Ahmad 1992:134). The modernist trope of the exile/nomad explains perhaps why these figures were so quickly assimilated into critical literature. They typified a mystified image of the male wanderer that already existed. In fact, a feminist interpretation of theories of migrancy questions this assumption of a gendered language of mobility. It seems that just as women were acceding to theory, male theorists seemed to take to the road (Wolff 1993:234). Perhaps theories of migrancy are nothing but a male exclusionary move within academe. Anyone who read Kerouac as an adolescent recognizes the erotic subtext of male travel narratives, whether they be literal or metaphorical, and how "being on the road" encodes potency and übermasculinity. An anarchic and antiquated romantic impulse in Western culture thus welcomes an Eastern strategy of migrancy and upward mobility. The theoretical "dharma bum" differs from his predecessor only by virtue of the fact that he must emigrate in order to reach his full potential.

The poststructuralist image of the Self was also indebted to the modernist terror of inner fragmentation. In Derridean postmodernism, social disconnectedness is not merely acknowledged but embraced; the impossibility of totality is celebrated as is the partial plural nature of human consciousness. Deconstruction conceives the world as a playful text and legitimizes the pleasures of nonattachment and noncommitment (Ahmad 1992:129). Modernism, with its romanticization of the intellectual exile, and deconstruction, with its affection for the fragmented Self,[2] thus set the stage for the creation of the third-world metropolitan elite exile.

There are two types of exile presented in the work of Edward Said—the actual and the metaphorical. They tend to be interchangeable. The real exile "is one of the saddest fates ... being a sort of permanent outcast, someone never at home, and always at odds with the environment, inconsolable about the past, bitter about the present and the future. There has always been an association between the idea of the exile and the terror of being a leper, a social and moral untouchable" (Said 1994:47). Exiles are unlike refugees who are political and innocent people requiring urgent care, expatriates who voluntarily live in a foreign country, or émigrés who have an ambiguous status. The exile carries with it a touch of solitude and spirituality (Said 2000:181). Said noted that exile is a strangely compelling and terrible experience. It is an unhealable rift forced between a human being and a native place, between the Self and its true home. Its essential sadness can never be surmounted (Said 2000:173). Although the exile can experience "heroic, romantic, glorious, even triumphant episodes," they appear as no more than efforts to overcome "the crippling sorrow of estrangement. The achievements of the exile are permanently undermined by the loss of something left behind forever" (Said 2000:173). They are "always eccentrics who feel their difference as a kind of orphanhood" (Said 2000:182). At this point, Said's depiction of exile is poignant and valid.

It is when he extends his definition to include those who "can share in the benefits of exile as a redemptive motif" (Said 2000:182–83) that a problem of representation arises. Said effectively elided the metropolitan intellectual with the exile, creating an exaggerated persona who is ideologically noble, victimized, and worthy of receiving sympathy. In "Third World Intellectuals and Metropolitan Culture," this exilic figure becomes the most authentic embodiment of the postcolonial intellectual. When Said claimed that exiles feel "an urgent need to reconstitute their broken lives, usually by choosing to see themselves as part of a triumphant ideology or a restored people" (Said 2000:177), he suggested that the politically committed can also claim exile status. Thus Said's advocacy for Palestinian rights made him a bona fide exile, even if other objective criteria were lacking.

In Said's metaphorization, exile becomes a "scrupulous subjectivity" to be cultivated (Said 2000:184), not a fate imposed on one by misfortune. It is a life that is willingly led outside the habitual order, not a forced *dépaysage*. It is "nomadic, decentered, contrapuntal" (Said 2000:186). Such exiles can choose to be "nay-sayers," individuals at odds with their society, never "fully adjusted, always feeling outside the chatty, familiar world . . . inhabited by natives." Said's metaphoric exile can opt "to avoid . . . the trappings of accommodation." Intellectual exile is "restlessness, movement, constantly being unsettled, and unsettling others" (Said 1994:52–53). The intellectual exile is someone "happy with the idea of unhappiness, so that dissatisfaction bordering on dyspepsia, a kind of curmudgeonly disagreeableness becomes a style of thought" (Said 1994:53). For Said, the exile is a model for the intellectual who needs not be an actual immigrant or expatriate but who, at will, "can think as one." Said's intellectual exiles can investigate "in spite of boundaries and always moving away from the centralizing authorities toward the margins, where you see things that are usually lost on minds that have never traveled beyond the conventional and the comfortable" (Said 1994:63). They are privileged characters, endowed with a messianic aura, individuals in touch with the "marginal and undomesticated." These intellectuals represent a certain contemporary ideal: they are "unusually responsive" to the traveler rather than the potentate, to the provisional and risky rather than the habitual, to the innovative and experimental rather than the authoritatively given status quo (Said 1994:63–64).

Said presents two possible positions for inhabiting the academic and cultural space provided by the university. On the one hand, we can be there in order to reign and hold sway. In this position, the academic professional is king and potentate. In this space, we sit surveying all before us with detach-ment and mastery. Our legitimacy is derived from the fact that we inhabit our own domain, which we can describe with authority as principally Western, African, Islamic, American, or whatever. The other possible position, although no less serious, is considerably more mobile and playful. To characterize this position, Said chose the image of the traveler, someone who depends not on power but on motion, on a willingness to go into different worlds, use different idioms, and understand a variety of disguises, masks, and rhetorics. The exile epitomizes the traveler rather than the potentate and, according to Said, is the model for the intellectual. In "Identity, Authority and Freedom: the Potentate and the Traveler," this migrant/traveler incarnates academic freedom (Said 2000:385–404).

Said privileges the exile as an iconoclast, someone who is exceptional, at odds with the rank and file. This exile is, not surprisingly, someone rather like Said envisioned himself to be. In "Intellectual Exile: Expatriates and Margin-als," Said identifies the exile as someone who "jolts" people (Said 1994:56). "The exilic intellectual does not respond to the logic of the conventional but to the audacity of daring, and to representing change, to moving on, not standing still" (Said 1994:64). The exile is "cosmopolitan . . . ironic, skeptical, even playful, but not cynical" (Said 1994:60–61).[3] Moreover, the intellectual is justified in assuming the persona of the exile because academe offers its professional class the opportunity "to discover and travel among other identi-ties" (Said 2000:403). Academic freedom provides an "invitation to give up one identity in the hope of understanding and perhaps even assuming more than one" (Said 2000:403–04). Since "modern Western culture is in large part the work of exiles, émigrés, refugees" (Said 2000:173), Said saw no problem in his and other intellectuals assuming these personae. The real is equivalent to its simulacrum.

The problem with Said's depiction of the intellectual as covert defector from societal values is that this image is nearly a perfect inversion of the actual situation. The academics' mental reservations regarding allegiance to institutions that offer them a privileged existence justifies their *anomie,* compromising their ability to defend civil values or even uphold basic fairness. Many such intellectuals eagerly comply with every abuse of a more vulnerable member of the academic community who can, indeed, never be innocent or a victim since he or she constitutes a representation of an enemy culture. This pattern of behavior explains to a great extent what really occurs in the adversarial and custodial university environment.

In theory, however, marginality, lack, victimization, and subalternity can be assimilated indiscriminately into the figure of the exile without having to elaborate sociopolitical hierarchies of class, race, or gender within postcolonial cultures and institutional settings. The only problem is that when nonvictims of displacement adopt a rhetoric of exile, they make themselves analogous to real victims of displacement. When they identify their rather comfortable existences with the likes of those who have suffered considerable hardships, they empty words such as *diaspora* and *exile* of their pain (Krishnaswamy 1995:128). No matter. We have reached such a stage of false consciousness that one can pretend to be a disenfranchised refugee, even if one spends one's youth playing the piano in elegant apartments above embassies. If one sees oneself as exceptional, one can be an exile without ever being exiled. In fact, being entitled is almost a prerequisite to being a postmodern exile. The poet Pierre Joris bases his theory of nomadic poetics on his middle-class European parents' peripatetic first-world travels. Because of his privileged childhood vacations, he claims the status of exile.

Sir Salman Rushdie has also embraced the figure of the exile. In *Imaginary Homelands* (Rushdie 1991a:10), Rushdie characterizes the exile as someone haunted by a sense of loss. Rushdie's exile creates fictions, not actual but invisible cities or villages, "imagining homelands, Indias of the mind." He prioritizes the geographically/culturally displaced writer as someone uniquely equipped both to reclaim the faded contours of a specific lost homeland and speak of things that have no universal significance (Krishnaswamy 1995:135). Rushdie claims that in order to see clearly, one has to cross a frontier (Rushdie 1991b:125). In fact, the migrant is perhaps the only species of human being who is free of the shackles of nationalism. It is a burdensome freedom (Rushdie 1991b:124). Rushdie presents a mythology of migrancy as a politics of opposition. Not only does he endow the migrant sensibility with the freedom and facility to construct its own contingent truths, but it becomes the single repository of experience as well as resistance (Krishnaswamy 1995:126).

Rushdie uses spiritual or mystic vocabulary to describe this migrant sensibility, emphasizing psychological processes over the political or sociological (Krishnaswamy 1995:132). In rather abstract terms, Rushdie reads the frontier from the margin in order to make migrancy a shared existential experience to which he and others like him have access. These individuals, who have "been forced by cultural displacement to accept the provisional of all truths, all certainties, have perhaps had modernism forced" upon them (Rushdie 1991a:12). In this image of the migrant, Rushdie also includes what he terms "internal exiles," such as women in patriarchies, minorities in hegemonic cultures, and oppressed majorities under occupation. By presenting the migrant as atypical *and* representative, unique *and* universal, Rushdie elaborates a strategic process of exclusion-inclusion.

Bharati Mukherjee has contrasted Rushdie's vision of immigration, a net gain despite its losses and confusions, to that of Naipaul, where the immigrant

only experiences loss and is driven to mimicry (Mukherjee 1989:11; cited in
Krishnaswamy 1995:138). We can similarly contrast Naipaul's mimicry to that
championed by Homi Bhabha,[4] who views mimicry as a form of empowerment. Unlike the exile/nomad of theory, Naipaul's migrant is not idealized:
quite the contrary. Naipaul stresses the psychological wounds of exile. His
mimic men are maimed as are their observers. Unlike Said's lyrical evoca-
tion of this figure, Naipaul's migrant is not presented as a positive (noble,
courageous) figure inhabiting the proper ideological space. Said's migrant,
quite simply, travels on a one-way ticket (Boer 1996:20). In terms of this
unidirectionality, Said's theory of exile is much like his theory of Orientalism. Just as in Orientalism, the East was uniformly acted upon, unable by the
constraints of imperial power to effect any significant agency or syncretism, so
too in "Traveling Theory," the exilic critic/theorist moves alone, taking theory
with him or her. Nothing is perceived as germinating in those third-world
sites without the intervention of the critic who has access to the outside
world. The exile becomes the necessary conduit for understanding the postcolonial condition and postcolonialism, once again, the only productive site
for resistance. Just as postcolonial criticism privileges the critic's subjectivity
and sanctions his cooptation of spokespersonship for the subaltern, so too
can the exile be configured.

An excellent example of just such a process can be seen in an essay in
the Bernheimer Report of 1995. In her contribution to this volume on the
state of the discipline, Emily Apter identifies comparative literature's colonial
legacy as manifested in its European-based emphasis rather than its commitment
to minority discourses. Although many comparatists are, in fact, Europeanists,
all are not. Among the ranks of comparatists, one does find Asianists and
Africanists. Some of us have followed Etiemble's advice and learned at least
one non-Western language and literature. But, just like the English department
monolinguist who champions multiculturalism, so here we have a comparatist
trained only in Western literatures bemoaning the Eurocentrism of comparative literature. This faulty premise—that comparative literature is continental, and comparatists are scholars who limit their comparisons to Western
cultures—allows this critic to juxtapose such comparatists with postcolonial
critics whom she sees as producing "the subject as complexified, pulled back
from the stereotype or positive image, deferred and postponed in transnational,
translational, transsexual and transtechnological space" (Apter 1995:90). Apter
clearly views the postcolonial critic's striving for identity retrieval and agency
as a form of empowerment for people of color.

This is, at best, a questionable premise, yet Apter goes further. She
views the exile of Leo Spitzer and the postwar generation of comparatists as
having had the same political urgency as someone like Homi Bhabha. The

Nazi-fleeing exile and the postcolonial elite, therefore, have the same exilic
consciousness (Apter 1995:94). The heated reactions to the 1993 Bernheimer
Report are in Apter's view a contest over who can lay claim to the exilic
aura of comparative literature's distinguished past (Apter 1995:94). Apter may
be correct in viewing the quest for a nomadic, exilic, migrant identity within
academe and theory as a border war, but not in the way that she envisions.
In a rather revolting metaphor, Apter equates the turf wars of the "new
arrivals," the metaphorical exiles and migrants such as the "Deconstructionists, Feminists, gay and lesbian studies, film and popular culture scholars and
postcolonial critics" with the legal battles of undocumented workers, illegal
aliens, and permanent residents (Apter 1995:94). Some cabal of Eurocentric
comparatists act as a border patrol to thwart these new arrivals. Like second-
and third-generation immigrants who supposedly abuse the latest arrivals
in town (an oddly prejudicial notion for a cosmopolitan scholar!), so too
these Eurocentric comparatists (some of whom may, in fact, be the forced
exiles of the last generation) mistreat the new theorists. The problem with
this analogy is clear: the real mistreatment and marginalization suffered by
immigrants to a new land and illegal aliens are not the same as the professional slights received by scholars in academe. While Apter may claim that
respective power structures want to keep out both new immigrants and new
theorists, the analogy is in very poor taste. Immigrant populations, particularly
the uneducated and untrained, do, in fact, suffer in ways that are not com-
mensurate with that of an educated elite. Nor are, as any perusal of the MLA
job listings for the past twenty years shows, deconstructionists, feminists, gay
and lesbian studies, film and popular culture scholars, and postcolonial critics
the marginalized victims of abuse that Apter would have us believe. If they
were, they could not rise from their shackles and claim their place "whether
continental comparatists like it or not," making comparative literature "more
interesting" (Apter 1995:94–95).

Apter envisions comparative literature as a field haunted by the recurrent
scenario of eviction and forced emigration. Its early history in the United
States is, in fact, tied to an exilic consciousness shaping its critical paradigms
and providing a kind of overarching historical paradigm for the ontology of
the discipline (Apter 1995:86). However, this exilic consciousness is different
from the exile that now haunts the field for the very reason that European
Jewish scholars fleeing Nazi persecution or Eastern Europeans fleeing Com-
munism are different from third-world elites who choose to come to the
States to attend Ivy-League institutions. However, the theories of migrancy
that we have examined in these pages enable this privileged class of voluntary
immigrants to covet victim status. In a cooperative venture with the white

academic power structure, these exilic "victims" usurp the suffering of those historically victimized for whom affirmative action was instituted. Theories of migrancy thus aim at undermining affirmative action.

The critical theory of exile is complicit with hegemonic postmodern theorizations of power and identity (Krishnasawmy 1995:127–28). All these discussions about borders, peripheries, margins, and centers are nothing but smokescreens for academic strategies of control. Perhaps the humanities do resemble the prison system as Barbara Harlow has suggested (Slemon 1992–93:154). Both are committed to the manufacture of responsibly culpable individuals whose position in the world economy is entirely a matter of their own self-fashioning. Upon examining the recent critical theories of alterity, one realizes the extent to which they are constructed less in order to understand the Other than to provide the theorist with an attractive, profitable, and engaged self-concept.

Poststructuralist discourses of alterity (whether they be multiculturalism, postcolonial theory, nomadology, traveling theory, exilic space, hybridity, or migrancy, etc.) enter institutionalized disciplines and circulate as theaters for naked careerism and self-emplacement (Slemon 1992–93:154). The institutional imperative is to elide what must at times be obvious to everyone involved: the academy is based on relationships that are identical to and, indeed, a consequence of imperialist impulses (Srivastava 1995:17). All this talk of empire does not occlude the petty little power plays, end-runs, and self-empowerment motivating this discourse. We must not lose sight of the fact that those very individuals who position themselves as victims are, indeed, Western-style and -trained mediators of cultural commodities, wholly owned subsidiaries of Euro-American publishers, readers, and universities (Krishnaswamy 1995:125). Appiah was justified in calling them a "comprador intelligentsia" (Appiah 1992:348). The salutary trope of the exile that we encounter among many poststructuralist critics valorizes the experiences of a few intellectuals who have gained access to privileged Western institutions by virtue of their wealth, class, and/or academic background. In their discourses of victimhood, they conflate their privileged experiences with those of disenfranchised underclass immigrants (Behdad 2000:82).

Most immigrant intellectuals are not forced exiles but voluntary self-exiles. There is something unsavory about professional spokespersons for the diaspora appropriating the victimization of the forced exile, when their moments of departure were too comfortable and too autonomous to use these terms. The forced exile's situation should not be made analogous to the relative comfort of the intellectual immigrant's voluntary self-exile. Even though postcolonial theory downplays the unequal relations within third-world societies it purports to study (Dirlik 1997:37), the class and gender differences among immigrant intellectuals and migrant labor, economic refugees, and political exiles should not be erased.

What becomes strikingly clear is that migrancy mavens are primarily interested in investigating themselves as third worlders and their relationship to the first world. Chinua Achebe notes that the hemispheres follow different standards both financially and figuratively (Achebe 2000:92). The market economy that frees a Kwame Anthony Appiah to celebrate global mobility and its freedom to elect the local forms of human life within which to live (Appiah 1997) does not empower the unfree nonmetropolitan third world. The intellectual exile possesses a freedom of self-creation unavailable to most other people. Here again, we have a problem of representation. First, there was the myth of the voiceless subaltern, and now the metaphoric exile robs the forced exile of his voice of protest. It is particularly revealing that these theorists of exile virtually ignore those whose existences are so miserable as to preclude ever becoming real exiles, let alone metaphorical exiles.

It seems quite clear that the metaphorization of exile is a strategy of empowerment within first-world academe that betrays a class/caste crisis. By divesting the Other of its specificity, postcolonial criticism neutralizes complex local histories and culturally specific knowledges into versions of postmodern diversity (Krishnaswamy 1995:129) where class hierarchies are occluded. Once class privilege is self-consciously erased through parody or irony, it is possible for third-world elites to align themselves with less privileged members of the immigrant population. Thanks to Spivak, they have already been able to legitimize themselves as authentic spokespersons for entire groups of dispossessed immigrants.

Bharati Mukherjee offers a plausible explanation for this need to appropriate the space of the disenfranchised. She sees it resulting from a "loss of face meltdown" (Mukherjee 1989:11), when immigrant intellectuals must face the grim facts of racism. Their Eurocentrism does not involve them floundering among disempowered minorities. In "An Invisible Woman," she describes how this privileged group has struggled, worked hard, and been rewarded. They are not equipped, however, to accept any proof of their unworthiness (Mukherjee 1981:36, 38; cited in Krishnaswamy 1995:133). In societies without set rules of caste, the deck is not stacked in their favor. Under the metaphors of hybridity, migrancy, and exile, third-world intellectuals recoup some of the power they feel they have lost. Embracing their subalternity with the oppressed, third-world intellectuals can recapture their preimmigrant power and privilege. The semantics of subalternity and its oppositional stance thus contribute to an upward mobility within their new "exilic" space. They get hired as nonminority minorities teaching victimhood with their class arrogance rehabilitated.

Theories of migrancy, assimilable to dominant postmodern ideology, enable upper-class professionals whose immigration was fundamentally voluntary to assume a noble and poignant position. The compulsion to make inflated claims is symptomatic of the discursive space in which third-world intellectuals choosing to live in the first world function and how the third world is conceived and consumed (Krishnaswamy 1995:128). These essentially nonvictimized victims usurp the pain of others when they claim that the diaspora designates equally the nineteenth-century Indian indentured workers in Trinidad and Fiji as well as twentieth-century Indian scientists, professors, and surgeons in America (Nelson 1992:x; cited in Krishnaswamy 1995:128). In the classroom, we are left with such grotesqueries as Filipino contract workers being written as Saidian exiles (Constable 1997) endowed with contrapuntal visions (San Juan 2002:186).

THE NOMAD

Critical discussion celebrating the nomad is flourishing in a way similar to that of its theoretical *Doppelgänger,* the exile. Professional conferences regularly devote panels and workshops to this theme. The nomad is at least as hot a commodity as the exile. Like the exile, interest in the nomad as a critical trope is due to recent theoretical trends that problematize notions of identity. The nomad is also not a new figure but rather a reworking of an old trend that is experiencing a renaissance in critical circles, the field of nomadology. The nomad actually has a considerable pedigree with a number of theorists having contributed to its formation. In *Origines de l'Occident* (Giraud-Boura 1972), nomadism is defined as a refusal to be domesticated and an openness to the world and its curiosities. The nomad appears in a state of spiritual becoming, as opposed to the material rootedness of the nonnomad. The nomad represents a dynamic and renewing force, the bearer if not of positive knowledge then of existential feeling.

Jean Duvignaud analyzed nomadic existence from a psychological perspective (Duvignaud 1975). He presented nomadic desire as pure, unsublimated, and direct in its realization. The nomad, not hampered by ideological constraints, possesses a spiritual fluidity. On a socioeconomical level, the nomad does not share in the construction of the state, nor does he even subscribe to the notion of the "nation." The nomad does not contribute to a market economy but exchanges goods through potlatch. Ironically, Duvignaud, who years earlier had accused Lévi-Strauss of nostalgia in his depiction of tribals in *Tristes tropiques,* idealizes the nomad, seeing him standing outside what this critic views as the vicious circle of production and consumption, not bound by any fixed concepts. Duvignaud positions the nomad as existing always outside of codes and unwilling to accept any discourse of closure. As such, Duvignaud's nomad constitutes a utopian model for the future.

The poet Kenneth White employed the term *intellectual nomadism* as a state of objectivity, where one seeks to enter into relationships with all varieties of individuals and make them cherished objects of study and one's intellectual property. White claimed to borrow this formulation of intellectual nomadism from Ralph Waldo Emerson. White maintained that Emerson spoke of the intellectual nomad who traverses all latitudes while being true to himself, like Kalmouk in relation to his Khan. Taking this concept of the 'nomad' as the point of departure for his study of the nomadic spirit, White was particularly interested in the relationship between exterior wandering and interior law.

Perhaps the best known theory of the nomad (at least for literary critics) is to be found in the work of Gilles Deleuze; particularly in the essay "Pensée nomade" of *Nietzsche aujourd'hui?* and in the chapter, coauthored with Félix Guattari, entitled "Traité de nomadologie" of *Mille plateaux.* Deleuze and Guattari presented nomads as people existing outside history, whose geography is to be found in smooth space (*espace lisse*), beyond the control of the rational and administrative machine (Deleuze and Guattari 1980:447–50).[5] Nomads are war machines—raiding, looting, and killing sedentary populations. Deleuze and Guattari characterized nomads as not necessarily always on the move. They can travel in place. In other words, their notion of the nomad was not historically that of the migrant. The nomad takes up the nomadic life in order to stay in the same place *and* escape codes. For Deleuze and Guattari, nomadic thought is a way "to conceive of individuality free from the confines of identity" (Miller 1998:179). They viewed it as a cure for all the ills attendant on capitalism, among which is identity. As Brian Massumi presents their reasoning in his introduction and translation of *Mille plateaux,* nomadic thought synthesizes a multiplicity of elements without effacing that heterogeneity (Miller 1998:174).[6] Nomadic thought is affirmative, even when its apparent object is negative (Deleuze and Guattari 1987:xiii).[7] It is based on notions of constant deterritorialization.

Deleuze's concept of the nomad inspired Rosi Braidotti to devote a volume to the topic of nomadic subjectivity. Braidotti claims that the nomad enacts transitions without a teleological purpose (Boer 1996:9). She presents the nomad "as a style of thought that evokes or expresses ways out of a phallocentric vision of the subject" (Braidotti 1994:8). The nomad is a figuration or style (Braidotti 1994:8) that foregrounds transdisciplinarity (or Deleuze's notion of deterritorialization) and a mixing of various ways of speaking. Nomadic style also entails a continuous critique of the concept of the 'unified subject.' It proposes alternative or multiple subjectivities. It involves transformations and transitions without predetermined destinations or lost homelands. The nomad has fixed trajectories, and thus returns with incredible regularity (Braidotti 1994:22, 25). Braidotti's figuration of the nomad also implies an existential mode of being and a polyglot who lives in between languages. The nomad assumes a skeptical stance concerning identities that are thought to be stable. Representing mobile diversity, its identity is an inventory of traces (Braidotti 1994:14, 35). For Braidotti, the nomad moves through established categories and levels of experience, "blurring boundaries without burning bridges" (Braidotti 1994:4). Since the individual who becomes a nomad is a man or woman of ideas (Braidotti 1994:13), Braidotti summons feminists and intellectuals to develop their nomadic consciousness. One is not born a nomad but needs to cultivate this persona (Boer 1996:10).

Another critical emplotment of the nomad appears in the notion of nomadic poetics. Pierre Joris defines nomadic poetics as a rhizomatic method, differing from collage, that writes in all or any languages (Joris 2003:5). Since the nomadic poet moves like a *comet* (Joris 2003:26), nomadic poetics is understood as a war machine, always on the move, always changing, morphing, moving through languages, cultures, terrains, and times without stopping. Joris describes nomadic writing as eschewing syntax and its hierarchical clausal structures. Writing proceeds nomadically by paratactic relations between terms producing concatenations held together (and simultaneously separated) either by pure spatial metonymical juxtapositions or by the play of the conjunctions *and* or *of* (Joris 2003:116). Simply put, writing is nomadic, when it is unhampered by the sedentarizing effects of normative grammar, syntax, and discursive forms (Joris 2003:115). It is writing that lacks punctuation marks (Joris 2003:118).

Joris likens nomadicity to gypsy argots and tricks. To this effect, he cites Georgio Agamben and the parallel he draws between Gypsy-argot and nomadicity. Agamben takes the traditional ideology of gypsy-argot and turns it on its head by suggesting that all "so-called" peoples are gypsies,[8] and all languages are dialects. Joris sees Agamben's reading as corresponding to Deleuze's and Guattari's concepts of nomadology and minor literatures as well as with what he calls nomadic poetics (Joris 2003:102–03). To supplement such speculation, Joris concludes his book with what we might assume to be an articulation of the nomadic poetics he has been theoretically defining throughout the volume. He and several university colleagues talk about themselves and their sense of alienation from academe and the world as white, male, educated professionals. These pages offer, perhaps, the clearest exposition of what Joris actually means by nomadic poetics. The nomad is a theoretical construct that allows the critic to talk about himself as a text.

The nomad has become an attractive metaphor for the critic's self-fashioning. Like the metropolitan exile, the nomad moves from the periphery to the metropolitan center and is at home everywhere and nowhere. The nomad is a person who is no longer disempowered by "cultural schizophrenia" and confined within collectivities such as a race, class, or nation. Like the postcolonial subject, the nomadic intellectual "writes back" to the European in the name of all the dispossessed and thus gains legitimacy in the international media market (Krishnaswamy 1995:125–26). The nomad also fits nicely into postmodernism's concern with hybridity and sites of ambivalence and its attempt to link dispersed groups or diasporic peoples across ruptures of space, time, nation, or language. According to the cultural studies scholar Lawrence Grossberg, postmodernism demands a nomadic subjectivity. Since cultural critics are never separated from their intellectual practices, they become cotravelers with nomads (Nelson and Grossberg 1988:388–89). Individuality can only function and be articulated out of a nomadic wandering through ever-changing positions and apparatuses (Nelson and Grossberg 1988:38). Grossberg defines nomadic subjectivity as amoebalike, having a shape that is always determined by "nomadic articulations" and is always itself effective (Nelson and Grossberg 1988:39). Such is the specificity of these definitions.

Gender, race, and ethnicity are just no longer satisfactorily inclusive categories for many critics. The nomad epitomizes what certain critics feel represents a need for new alignments that challenge fundamentally such static notions of identity. Notions of mobility, fluidity, provisionality, and process are deemed preferable to stasis and fixity. In cultural criticism of the late twentieth century, only ideologies and vested interests "fix" meaning. It is the job of cultural critics to destabilize those meanings (Wolff 1993:228). Cultural studies, with its concern for hybridity and its mandate to excavate the heterogeneous invented roots of identity, provided one response to the perceived bankruptcy of traditional paradigms. The nomad provides yet another model. In the quest for an alternative beyond identity, a postidentitarian model, the critical trope of the nomad, an identity free from the constraints of identitarianism, becomes an ideal alternative, especially since these depictions of nomadic subjectivity are sufficiently vague and nonthreatening (Probyn 1990:184).

The above summary of theoretical discussions on the nomad is not intended to be exhaustive. It is presented, rather, to suggest the extent to which the nomad has a place within critical discourse. Contrary to one critic's judgment that critical formulations of the nomad should not even be taken seriously (Kaplan 1987:187–98), I believe that these theoretical nomads illuminate a central thesis of this volume—how critical depictions of alterity are far less concerned with improving our understanding of the Other and more concerned with constructing viable and prestigious notions of the Self. The nomad of nomadology wonderfully reflects poststructuralism's concern with and legacy of identitarian politics. The nomad is presented to postmodern audiences as the preeminent interpreter of the postcolonial reality (Krishnaswamy 1995:127) primarily because this figure expresses notions of intellectual freedom of movement and escape from ideology and bourgeois values. This role explains, perhaps, why the nomad appears in so many theoretical discussions. It also suggests why the nomad functions only metaphorically and why no care is given to specific discussions of actual nomads or any grounding in concrete reality. The project of nomadology has nothing to do with real and actual nomads because they are not important; only the critic has significance. As one scholar notes, the only real nomads in nomadology are Deleuze, Guattari, and their fellow travelers (Miller 1998:177). In much the same manner as Spivak's subaltern, nomads appear as inert objects, existing only to be represented by the critic. The subaltern's presumed voicelessness gives authority to a Spivak to represent them, just as the absence of any citation from African or Asian oral or written nomadic sources (Miller 1998:176) justifies our need for Deleuze and Guattari. The critic's voice and self-representation eclipse the actuality of the Other. As Stephan Muecke notes, Deleuze's and Guattari's presentation of nomadology in *Mille plateaux* "enables us to take on board the concept 'nomad' without having recourse to anthropological definitions which would only reintegrate the concept of the body or anti-nomadic thinking" (Miller 1998:180). Their construction of the nomad confers on them a certain immunity by allowing them to stand outside the suspect domain of manipulation and representation (Miller 1998:178). The same might be said for all the theorists of the Other examined in these pages.

However, it cannot really be said that Deleuze and Guattari eschew anthropology. In fact, they quote many anthropologists, and anthropology is nothing, if not representational (Miller 1998:180). The project of Deleuze and Guattari in *Mille plateaux* actually requires ethnographic authority. Their scholarly apparatus is deceptive. As Christopher Miller shows, their entire endeavor creates a need to make assertions about cultures around the world.[9] They use anthropology in two ways. They cite anthropologists, and they make anthropological statements of their own. They pretend that nomadic thought is free and rhizomorphous, but it is actually representational and arborescent;

it follows the practices of a violently representational colonial ethnography at the same time that it is claiming to be anticolonial, antiauthoritarian, and nonrepresentational (Miller 1998:181–82). Similarly, in those instances where Deleuze and Guattari "do" anthropology themselves, their discourse is full of judgments and characterizations, complicated by their ambivalence to such things and their constant claims that their work is alien to representation and identity construction (Miller 1998:187). The wide-ranging nature of *Mille plateaux* demands the very anthropological information that is in direct contradiction to the supposedly nonauthoritative nature of their work.[10] Deleuze and Guattari compound their methodological difficulties by a willingness to make assertions about cultural practices based on very uneven and exoticizing source materials (Miller 1998:196). Their reliance on such material raises an important question. To what degree is the whole concept of nomadic discourse not a venture into exoticism?

The theoretical nomad functions as do the other discourses examined in these pages that purport to engage the Other. It presents a means of observing the Self and reaffirming one's own position. The nomad appears in theory as the armature on which the theorizing Self is sculpted. Like the Other of multiculturalism and postcolonialism, its presence speaks of sociopolitical privilege and artistic self-indulgence. A subject passing from plural individualization to a singularized quasiallegorical condition (becoming-animal, becoming-minoritarian, and becoming-third world) is a masquerade invented expressly for white male majoritarian humans to play and, as such, is a form of exoticism (Miller 1998:192).

That nomadological theory does not reflect actual reality should not surprise us. We have long since learned not to expect literary theory to reflect sociopolitical reality. But we are not so jaded as readers not to expect that theory should illuminate literature. The question then becomes: what insights, if any, does the critical emplotment of the nomad bring to our understanding of literary theory? It is clear that we have come to the point in criticism where we do not even question why a theory called "nomadology" fails to deal with the actuality of nomads. It is deemed legitimate to appropriate and use the nomad without feeling the necessity of speaking of or to real nomads. This is a fundamental problem, especially for those branches of literary theory that purportedly investigate identity and positionality.

Poststructural theory claims an interest in reality. It deciphers the very power structures that art occludes. Literary critics demand that literature's representations of the Other be unmasked and the systemic limits that they place on representation be revealed as hegemonic. It may well be the moment that theory demands at least as much of its own methodology. Perhaps the politics of theory manifested in the emplotment of the nomad as a critical trope needs to be deconstructed. I would venture to suggest that such self-interrogation is warranted, lest critical theory engender the same type of "resounding inconsequentiality" that Russell Berman has attributed to contemporary aesthetic production (Berman 1989:81).

At issue here is a failure to deal with the Other. The identitarian politics at work are blatant. The Amero-European critic theorizing the nomad, with real nomadic gypsies never far away, engages in exotic flights extolling life in smooth spaces with nonideological consciousness and exemplary freedoms. Here, we are in the realm of pure exoticism, where an identity is being established not of the Other but of the hypertrophied exoticizing Amero-European subject. However, it is the properties metaphorically accorded to this subject that are of interest. Theory, understood as symbolic capital and combined with spokespersonship, becomes even more a form of professional empowerment. The constructs of multiculturalism, postcolonialism, and nomadology have allowed critics to appear relevant on a global level. The real world and the variety of its peoples and their literatures are eclipsed by this larger form of professional empowerment.

A WAND'RING MINSTREL I,
A THING OF SHREDS AND PATCHES

If we define exoticism as a quest that does not terminate with the exploration of a particular culture but spins off in search of a different set of cultural elements in order to satisfy psychic and/or physical *Wanderlust* (Remak 1978:56), it does not fundamentally differ from nomadic thought as formulated by these theorists. Just as the exoticist never needs to write about real Others, so too the nomadologist is never accountable to tribes who have no permanent home. Critics can taste the romance of exile and can play at being diasporic, nomadic, or disenfranchised without having to dirty their hands. The critic can also claim to talk for the margin and, in doing so, pretend to speak from the margin, while actually inhabiting a space that is quite close to the center. Once again we see a deep-seated need to distance oneself from global capitalism. When critics appropriate the metaphorical space of the nomad, exile, and marginal, they hope to exonerate themselves for all the benefits they receive from this same capitalism.

The critic who possesses "nomadological immunity" can say anything, since nomadic thought does not immure itself in the edifice of an ordered interiority (Deleuze and Guattari 1987:xii). Deleuze and Guattari's pure idea of nomads is really no different from exotic representations in eighteenth- and nineteenth-century Orientalism. We may well have come to the point in time where theories of alterity do not differ from exoticism. The critics of Orientalism have constructed new orientalisms. Both the Orientalist and the nomadologist use the Other more as a pretext for self-investigation rather than examining the Other in a meaningful way. Both deal in abstraction, both are freed from the ethical burden of representing real Others or nomads who might actually have something to say. Orientalist exoticism can be defined in terms of a "lack," desire/disavowal, and failed hermeneutic (Figueira 1994). In both exoticism and pedagogies of alterity, the Other appears to fill a lack perceived by the metaphorical traveler/critic. Demarcating the Self from the Other motivates both encounters. Both are animated by an identifying submission to an idealized Other and a secret search for origins. The personal search involved in pedagogies of alterity is, however, much more calculated and driven by ideological concerns. There is no unconscious enthusiasm masking the lack.

Exoticism pivots around the binary of desire and disavowal, when reality does not live up to one's expectations. What I will term the "new critical exoticism" places desire on the level of the critic's need for validation. The multiculturalist and postcolonial critics position themselves not only to explicate but also to understand realities. Disavowal has nothing to do with a critic's complex over the realities not fitting one's expectations. Disavowal now functions as a form of "bracketing." Orientalist exoticism originates out of the priority given to the Other's inability to fulfill desire. Nomadological exoticism does not set such a priority. The agenda is elsewhere—not in the lack that animates the quest itself but in the reliance on the aesthetic in the form of theorizing for theory's sake. Texts usually recede from the horizon, leaving us with the critics and their messianic theorizations of movement and myths of self-aggrandizement. The minstrals of literary theory tune their supple songs to whatever changing humours a given critical situation demands.

Critics should face up to the consequences of the representational authority they assume and cease pretending to have no authority at all. They should abandon their delusion of nonauthority (Miller 1998:209). Sixty years ago, the great Dalit jurist Ambedkar framed the Indian constitution to limit the brahmin's right to speak for the outcaste. Why now have postcolonial critics been allowed to colonize the voice of the marginalized Other? As every good Indian Buddhist knows, brahmin authority, whether it be religious, political, or theoretical, does not necessarily lead to enlightenment.

CHAPTER 6

OCCIDENTALISM

The prologues are over. It is a question, now, of final belief. So, say that
final belief must be in a fiction. It is time to choose.

—Wallace Stevens, *The Palm at the End of the Mind*

THEORY CONFRONTS REALITY

In certain respects, Orientalist criticism has rewritten history. However, it has
done so only partially. It has provided a one-sided apologia regarding Western
sins and sinners without addressing the flip side. Examining the East to see if
it too might be cluttered with stereotypes or misconceptions has never been
a sustained part of this critique (Freund 2001:10). Moreover, there has been
little inquiry into the dehumanizing trends in the East toward itself and its
Other, the West. In its latter incarnation, colonial discourse analysis, pre- and
postcolonial societies are usually presented as sanitized, third-world equivalents of Arcadian idylls with scant attention paid to the historical integrity
of location. Indigenous practices of oppression and exploitation tend to be
overlooked in the homogenization of colonial sites. Time-honored corrupt
practices, nativist racism and sexism thus receive little scrutiny in postcolonial criticism. The focus of investigation has primarily been the past sins of
colonizers and the present-day threats from globalism. Thanks to Orientalism
and colonial discourse analysis, colonialism has to a certain extent become
an opportunity not a burden for postcolonial elites. Because of the evil of
colonialism in the past, the West has lost all rights in the present to address
any subject having to do with the East (Freund 2001:5). With regard to the
East, the West is permanently guilty and the East perpetually exonerated.

Postcolonial criticism has inherited these limitations from the Orientalist critique and developed some of its own, first and foremost, the exorbitant role assigned to the critic. Postcolonial criticism replaced the imperial consumer as the subject matter of Orientalist criticism, making the postcolonial critic him/herself the prime actor of the critique. Rather than examining the concrete empirical circumstances of postcolonial subjects still inhabiting these sites, this criticism focuses in large measure on theorists' claims to insight by virtue of their residing outside the locales in question. Postcolonial criticism thus no longer examined the culture's original Orientalist consumers, but postcolonial culture's contemporary interpreters (Freund 2001:7). We have come a long way from discussing nineteenth-century paintings of odalisques and harems, focusing instead on the contemporary critics themselves and what they see in such paintings.[1] It is no longer a question of revealing how a text codifies Eurocentric sexual or political superiority, but rather an examination of the contemporary critic's intellectual insecurity and alienation. We no longer investigate how the West has managed the East, but instead how postcolonial elites manage their relationship with the West (Freund 2001:8). Orientalist criticism's analysis of imperial fantasies has shifted to postcolonial criticism's examination of academic fantasies (Freund 2001:8).

The innovative value of Orientalist criticism was not, as many thought, its portrayal of obvious self-serving imperialist stratagems. Numerous critics before Said had done such work. What was new and significant was its close readings of contemporary political and cultural texts and examination of how imperialist abuses had transmuted into postcolonial subtleties that were no less damaging than imperialist justifications. However, this project of Orientalist criticism, which began as something constructive, became trivialized. As a consequence, the last twenty-five years spent deconstructing alterity and imposing Lacanian psychoanalysis on "readings of the Other" have not resulted in any greater understanding or marked improvement of relations. We have seen how multiculturalism allowed the West to feign study of the East. Postcolonialism permitted previously colonized countries to avoid confronting their own history in a critical fashion, while it focused on the numerous and real sins of the West. In fact, many third-world scholars have themselves become Orientalists, prompting some critics of postcolonial theory to question the degree to which the whole endeavor has become less a critique of Western power and more an apologia for Eastern failure and an intellectual adventure in rationalization. In the West, it has been enough to embrace guilt and complicity. In the East, it sufficed to condemn and feel victimized. It was never necessary to analyze the East's conflicted relationship to the West.

Postcolonial elites internalized Euro-American models and ideals as part of their self-fashioning and consolidation of power in much the same way that colonial elites had done before them (Figueira 2002). Under colonialism, Europeans had bequeathed to the privileged segments of society a state committed to the project of minimalizing the role of religion in culture. This elite embraced a liberal concept of 'secularization' as a key element of modernity, regardless of the fact that they would rule over and be accountable to largely religious nations (Lincoln 2003:64), whose populations see secularism as a Western imposition. Postcolonialism thus threatens the profanation of what is holy (Lincoln 2003:64) as much as colonialism ever had done. Postcolonial criticism borrowed from poststructuralist theory relativized conceptions of morality and reality that had served Western intellectuals so well when they had been confronted with Solzhenitsyn's books, Cambodian horrors, Solidarity, and 1989 (Lilla 2001:187). Language, previously used by colonizers to defend Western tyranny, could now be used by postcolonial subjects to ignore or excuse crimes committed by homegrown tyrants. In the East or West, theory can be enlisted to explain away any troubling sense of moral repugnance. This manipulation of language, spawned by the critique of logocentrism, was, perhaps, the greatest legacy that poststructuralist criticism handed down to us. This heritage was put into grand relief in the rhetoric that surfaced after September 11.

In what manner did multiculturalism and postcolonial studies as sciences of understanding the Other provide America with tools to understand or deal with the attacks on the World Trade Center and the Pentagon? It appears that during the very years that multiculturalism was extending its influence in academe, the study of foreign languages was dropping consistently.[2] There was always some sense that multiculturalism never translated itself into learning languages, history, and the literatures of foreign countries. Why would students, raised in the market-based university, bother to learn a language such as Arabic when consuming an exotic culture could be achieved by viewing its films with subtitles? No one was prepared, however, for the sad reality that the intercepted warnings of the potential terrorist attack had gone for years unread, for lack of available State Department translators. As Margaret Talbot has noted, American universities produced six students majoring in Arabic in 2001. After September 11, the State Department made a pathetic plea for citizens with knowledge of Pashto and Arabic to volunteer their services. Multiculturalism had not gotten Americans to study cultures in any real way, but terrorism would (Talbot 2001). In contrast to the failure of multiculturalism as a pedagogy, its ideological premises, along with those of postcolonialism, proved to be far more successful. In fact, multicultural and postcolonial rhetoric influenced significantly the manner in which the events of September 11 would be deconstructed.

What was noteworthy about the academic responses to September 11 was their lack of balance. There is nothing intrinsically wrong with criticizing the politics and activities of the United States. Such criticism is responsible, however, when equal time is given to the leadership in those countries purportedly victimized by America, whose politics are no less disastrous (Dirlik 1997:249–50). What was missing from the post–September 11 academic discussions was the critique both against the powers that dominate and shape the world *and* the reactionary culturalist responses that legitimize oppression. The absence of this double vision, I believe, reflected the influence of poststructuralism's critique of Euro- and logocentrism.

RHETORIC

Charles Paul Freund has noted how, in the aftermath to the September assault, Edward Said announced in *The Observer* that he felt that Islam was being blamed for the attacks (Freund 2001:1). Those of us who were glued to our televisions found this claim bizarre. After journalists had been far too hasty to speculate that the Oklahoma bombing had been perpetrated by Arabs rather than by the radical antigovernment individualist Timothy McVeigh, the press was very careful to ascribe no blame to any group. George Bush, not generally known for his religious subtlety, had taken great pains to dissociate the bombers of the World Trade Center from Islam. In many of his statements, Bush distinguished Islamic radicalism from what he termed "the true Islam of peace." Nevertheless, Said characterized the reaction to the attacks as anti-Islamic. In doing so, he relied on the familiar litany of Orientalist criticism: the media and the president had reacted monolithically to the East and Islam (Said 2001a:27). Whether Said thought that American policy should be blamed or was insufficiently blamed is not our concern. What is interesting, however, is that he chose to frame his comments along the lines of Orientalist binaries. The form in which he couched his argument—that any reaction to September 11 must follow an established paradigm—lends his comments legitimacy, even though this model may not represent the reality of the situation in an accurate way. The rhetoric of Orientalist criticism did, in fact, rally the troops.

A number of intellectuals and artists rose to the occasion. As Steven Erlanger noted in the *New York Times,* the very week that a new Broadway production of one of his *opera buffa* opened on Broadway, Dario Fo opined that the "great speculators wallow in an economy that every year kills tens of millions with poverty—so what is 20,000 dead in New York? Regardless of who carried out the mission, this violence is the legitimate daughter of the culture of violence, hunger and inhuman exploitation" (Erlanger 2001). The German composer Karlheinz Stockhausen called the attack on the World Trade Center "the greatest work of art imaginable for the whole cosmos" (cited in Erlanger 2001). Marie-Jose Mondzain, director of France's Centre Nationale de Recherches Scientifiques, wrote in *Le Monde*: "I . . . feel redoubled in me all the reasons to condemn a world that sings along with a catastrophic president who defends the death penalty and who has only disdain for the Middle East" (cited in Erlanger 2001). This rhetoric exhibited a marked empathy with mass murderers.

There was also the reaction of American academe. A Yale history professor claimed that America's military, economic, and diplomatic might and "offensive cultural messages *understandably provoked*" this hatred (cited in Hartocollis 2001; italics added). At Brown University, a curricular guide instructed professors to help students understand why people resented the United States. At a Haverford College Quaker meeting, America was deemed "the most violent nation of earth," and the participants were told that as Americans they were all complicit in the attack (Hartocollis 2001).[3] These commentators were at pains to show all the reasons why U.S. policy and behavior could provoke such an admittedly heinous attack. In this commentary, we encounter a principled avoidance of justifying mass murder while endorsing the basic assumptions regarding American guilt voiced by the most strident anti-U.S. critics.

As Arif Dirlik has noted, many radical responses followed a set pattern. They began with heartfelt expressions of dismay at the criminal acts. They then proceeded to catalog the injustices that the United States has visited upon the world, as if the latter were sufficient to explain what had happened and that such an explanation obviated the need for anything else. Although the perpetrators of the criminal acts had made no pretense of speaking in the name of the oppressed, those with ambivalent feelings toward the United States and its policies insisted that the world's resentment towards the United States must be taken seriously (Dirlik 2001:245). Rather than letting the acts speak for themselves, they were framed against the sorrier aspects of the American record abroad.

As Louis Menand noted, if France or Germany had been attacked without warning, one would not expect the world's response to focus on questioning the collective guilt of either nation (Menand 2002:98). Nevertheless, much of the discourse following September 11 held to the view that America is the global source of evil and deserved what happened. Proponents of this view

include Noam Chomsky (2001) and Arundhati Roy (2003). The terrorist
attacks were seen as "blowback" from the United States' role as the leading
terrorist state (Menand 2002:98). The metastasization of radical Muslims that
the United States had organized to trap the Soviets in a Vietnamlike quagmire
in Afghanistan had now turned upon their creator (Chomsky 2001). Menand
responded to Chomsky's argument by suggesting that the World Trade Center
attack should rather be seen as the extreme of the imaginable consequences
of the United States supporting an Afghan resistance movement in 1979. This
support can just as easily be interpreted as a consequence for participating in
global affairs (Menand 2002:98–99), but it was not read in this fashion. What
Chomsky saw as an inevitable outcome of the policy of 1979, Menand saw
more reasonably in my view as an extreme and unforeseeable result. There
was also some discussion of how Bin Laden should be viewed as an entirely
American creation, "modernity's demonic twin" (Menand 2002:101), not as
anything arising from Islamism, Wahabism, Saudi politics, or any number of
other sources. Also missing from these reactions to the September 11 events
was the recognition of how the terrorists themselves characterized their
actions. In the spirit of multiculturalism and postcolonialism, Bin Laden and
the terrorists must be understood through the lens of the West. Baudrillard
subscribed to this optic, when he opined that "we can say that the horror
for the 4000 victims of dying in those twin towers was inseparable from the
horror of living in them" (cited in Menand 2002:101). He was essentially
demanding that we interpret the victims' horrific deaths as equivalent to
bourgeois ennui. Their death can only be read in terms of their existences in
Western capitalist culture. Somehow we wished it upon ourselves, knowing how
global capitalism has systematically deprived us of access to the unmediated
and the real. Baudrillard attributed the destruction of the Twin Towers neither
to Islamicist terrorism nor to any act from "outside" but characterized it as
a sympathetic suicide from "within." The system generated its own suicide.
Here the blowback is not from military imperialism but from the economic
and cultural varieties. Menand points to the absurdity of Baudrillard's vision
of the event as an "internal equilibrating mechanism" (Menand 2002:101).
The individuals died because of having installed "global circulation." The
attack itself becomes a "terrorist situational transfer." On a moral and ethical
level, such an interpretation is simply obscene. On a critical level, however,
it struck a familiar chord.

     In such accounts and numerous others, we were presented with what
might be described as the flip side of Orientalism. The same reductionist
misrepresentation that the West had applied to the Arab world was now being
applied to America. As Freund noted in *Reason* (2001), such a monolithic

portrayal of America can be called "Occidentalism." In fact, the tropes of Occidentalism mirror those of Orientalism: in both, women are stereotyped as sexually rapacious, and men are consistently depicted as craven. Both the Orientalist and the Occidentalist view all East-West encounters as replays of the crusades. Both uncover conspiratorial regimes, whether in the form of Oriental despotism or of Zionism. Just as Orientalists once exculpated themselves for colonialism, so too do Occidentalists now exculpate themselves for Islamism (Freund 2001:16). The Egyptian feminist Nadje Al-Ali has devised a useful definition for the term *Occidentalism.* She sees it as a mode of representation that uses available cultural categories to gain symbolic advantages for the Self and handicap the Other. In this respect, Occidentalism fits the model we have established for the poststructuralist theories examined in this volume: their primary function is one of self-fashioning for the critic. As we might suspect, the stage for Occidentalism had been prepared by postmodernism's earlier efforts at relativizing fundamental philosophical and political premises. We have seen how in literary circles for some time facts and objectivity, understood as culturally constructed strategies of imperial control, are brack-eted. An intellectually and politically debilitating historicism assumes that most events need to be comprehended within the context of a history structured by capitalism and colonialism (Dirlik 2001:246), ignoring the fact that these two have individual histories and that they may not have the same meaning or same consequences at all times and places.

Postcolonialism added to this critique its own universal based on Orien-talist criticism: Western imperialism is always to blame. As Edward Rothstein opined in the *New York Times,* any act against the West by a postcolonial power cannot be viewed as anything but a reaction to a previous imperial act by the West. We cannot then condemn the World Trade Center attack, since Western hegemonic behavior is the fundamental cause of terrorism, and the United States, against which this act was directed, is the most powerful Western hegemonic power. The rhetoric of postcolonialism and its call for the rule of relativism enabled us to blame the victim and justify terror. Rothstein, a mere journalist, questioned whether such relativism should play any role in the face of destruction that called for a "transcendent ethical perspective" (Rothstein 2001). We, as readers of recent literary criticism, are usually far removed from such moral concerns. In fact, we might even find the logic in play here commonplace and conventional. What could be a more disturbing indictment of the state of theory today?

The Occidentalist rhetoric exhibited in these responses reflects the school of thought that views the United States as the source of all evils (from the price of beef in France to AIDS in Africa). This world vision offers certain advantages. For one, it allows some countries to avoid accepting responsibility for their actions (Revel 2003:61). By attributing all moral failings and grotesque intellectual errors to the United States as the monster scapegoat, certain nations can absolve themselves of their own moral errors and mistakes. If America becomes the Great Satan, all the little Satans pale in comparison. America can thus exist to console Europe and the world for its own failures (Revel 2003:158–59) among which we can count its complacency and indulgent complicity in Communist and post-Communist genocides.

We can compare and contrast this view of America with discussions taking place in academe in the days following the attacks. This narrative was compiled and published in a report of the American Council of Trustees and Alumni (ACTA). The stated purpose of the *ACTA Report* was to show to what extent the public response to the attacks differed from that of the academic rhetoric. The public had responded to September 11 with a clear condemnation, while ACTA claimed that many academics had failed to do so (Martin and Neal 2001:4). As we have seen, a number of academics placed blame for the attacks on American policies. ACTA not only compiled this academic commentary but went a step further in claiming that the disparity in responses between the public and the university sectors could be attributed to the moral relativism of recent academic trends.[4] It also drew a parallel between the attribution of the world's ills to Western civilization and the devaluation of Western civilization courses on the university level.

David Palumbo-Liu, an ardent multiculturalist, interpreted the report's analysis as a condemnation of the multicultural curriculum, especially its criticism of the "smorgasbord of often narrow and trendy classes and incoherent requirements that did not convey the great heritage of human civilization" (Martin and Neal 2001:5) that currently fill university catalogs (Palumbo-Liu 2002:124). The report did not directly associate this "smorgasbord" with multiculturalism but rather with the loss of survey courses in Western civilization. It called for the reinstatement and expansion of American history and Western civilization in university curricula. While it did not, contrary to Palumbo-Liu's claim, attack multiculturalism specifically, it did something far more "blameworthy." It "outed" academics who were accustomed to discoursing only among themselves or in the controlled arena of their classrooms. The *ACTA Report* quoted post–September 11 academic commentary and cited attribution. It was this revelation of academic discourse that caused an uproar and resulted in cries of McCarthyism. In its defense at airing academic responses to September 11, the report claimed that academic freedom did not mean freedom from criticism (Martin and Neal 2001:9). Criticism, moreover, did not limit free speech. It also noted that an atmosphere "increasingly unfriendly to the free exchange of ideas" prevailed in academe (Martin and Neal 2001:5). The *New York Times* simply called the report "repugnant." ACTA had no right to "attack" dozens of professors for having reacted to the terrorist attacks in ways it authors considered inappropriate.[5]

ACTA had clumsily misidentified the problem. Rather than being in the business of defending the Western classics and Eurocentrism, ACTA and dedicated humanists should criticize the trends of uninformed and unanalytical claims in recent critical theory that are made in the name of anti-imperialism, anti-Eurocentrism, multiculturalism, and antiracism (Chow 1995:47). In the aftermath of September 11, there was nothing wrong with adding classes on Islam and Asian cultures. The addition of such courses does not imply, as ACTA claimed, that America's failure to understand Islam was to blame (Martin and Neal 2001:6–7). Rather, it was how these courses are often taught. How many new courses on Islam have been added to American curricula aiming primarily at apologetics rather than providing substantive knowledge of Islam (Podhoretz 2002:37)? We might refer here to courses on the Islamic world (like one recently added to the comparative literature curriculum at a large Big Ten university) that are taught under the direction of scholars with no knowledge of Islam or Arabic. Perhaps, as in the case in question, a Lacanian scholar can bring interesting insights to our understanding of literatures of the Islamic world, but is this really legitimate or responsible? Such courses are only possible when the world is consumed in translation, using the tools of theory rather than historical, anthropological, religious, or linguistic knowledge. In such courses, the proper ideological space is "inhabited," knowing the subject matter in any substantive manner is of secondary importance.

It is not good that students learn nothing about American history, just as it is unacceptable that they are ignorant of world history. The problem is that ideology and theory have replaced texts of any sort, great Western as well as great Eastern texts. The *New York Times* was equally wrong for suggesting that professors are routinely punished in America for their political posturings in the classroom or in print. For all their shared histrionics, neither ACTA nor those calling themselves critical patriots offered any original or constructive responses to September 11.

The terms of the responses to September 11 were straightforward: either endorse the position of American innocence under attack by the third world or draw attention to the sociopolitical causes of Arab extremists and, in doing so, essentially blame the victims (Žižek 2002:50). This either/or formulation was inadequate. Rejecting such an opposition, Slavoj Žižek offered an alternative. Since each response alone was one-sided and false, he suggested that both positions be adopted simultaneously. He accepted the necessity of condemning terrorism but redefined and expanded its terms so that it will also include some American and other Western powers' actions (Žižek 2002:51). Žižek saw this to be the only ethical response. He felt it necessary to show solidarity with all victims rather than the "moralizing mathematics of guilt and horror" presented in many of the Leftist, European, and critical patriotic responses. Each individual is incomparable. Any reluctance to empathize with the September 11 victims and any thought that we need to qualify this empathy with empathy for others shows, in Žižek 's view, bad faith. It also exhibits an implicit patronizing and racist attitude, rather than a sympathetic approach to the third world (Žižek 2002:51–52). While Žižek finds the uncritical patriot narrative—innocence under fire—to be vain, he reserves the bulk of his scorn for the Europeans and U.S. leftists whom he finds scandalous. He felt that the unimaginable stupidities they voiced after September 11 were petty and miserable. He was offended by the mathematical comparisons between the September 11 victims and Holocaust fatalities and reminders that the United States had created the Taliban and Bin Laden (Žižek 2002:51).

Abstractions, such as those voiced by Baudrillard, are absurd; the terrorists are real (Žižek 2002). According to Žižek, America stands in opposition to the antimodernists who want capitalism and economic development without the social change and cultural permissiveness that it engenders. It was this capitalism of the simulacrum that attacked the capitalism of the "all too real." It was able to do so because of the systematic stereotyping and degradation of the West, Occidentalism. The capitalism of the simulacrum took planes filled with innocent travelers, including children, and used them as bombs to kill capitalists of the real, Hispanic and black, Muslim and Hindu, waiters and plumbers, as well as white, Jewish and Christian stockbrokers.

The Occidentalism of the post-September 11 rhetoric was, in part, a product of the unsubstantial character of postmodern academic criticism. Žižek concludes that the relatively trifling character of standard cultural studies critical topics becomes glaringly apparent (Žižek 2002:48–49) when compared with the death of thousands. He questions whether cultural studies scholars will stick to the same topics or take a risk and attempt to radicalize their stance. He claims that maintaining the frivolousness of their inquiries after September 11 is a direct admission that their fight against oppression is a fight only within first-world capitalism's universe. And, indeed, the volume entitled *9/11 in American Culture,* published by the next generation of University of Illinois cultural studies professionals, with contributions by gurus such as Cary Nelson and Henry Giroux, proves this point stunningly.

Of the fifty-two essays in this volume, thirty deal with where the contributing academics were, what they experienced, and how they read September 11 as narrative, poetics, and personal studies. It was an event that "forced" one scholar "inwards" (Denzin and Lincoln 2003:138). Cary Nelson claims that cultural studies can help promote a dialogue with Islam but does not say how this can be done or by whom (Denzin and Lincoln 2003:144). There is an essay devoted to how one cultural studies scholar thinks of Arabs in terms of American movies such as *Lawrence of Arabia*, *The Mummy*, *Abbot and Costello Meet the Mummy*, and so on. Bert from *Sesame Street* appears on a poster somewhere in the Middle East (Denzin and Lincoln 2003:132), prompting a discussion of the Disneyfication of the Arab world. The inanity of these essays in a volume devoted to the "qualitative inquiry" of September 11 tells us everything we need to know regarding the relevance of this mode of analysis. Nothing of real worth in the Muslim world is examined. In fact, the Arab world is not even addressed. What we have are the ruminations, superficial or merely idiosyncratic and self-referential, of a group of scholars who have nothing to say about Arabs or the countries they inhabit.

The academic schools of criticism we have examined in this volume are noteworthy for their focus on theoretical abstractions and popular cultural allusions rather than distinctive traits of the cultures in question. Like postcolonial theorists enthralled by the triumphant creed of hybridity, in post–September 11 academic discourse, the victims are people made up of incommensurable mobile and unstable parts (Majid 2002:11). Like postcolonial critics, post–September 11 theorists focused on Western imperialist projects, past and present.[6] Postcolonial theories of "hybridity, homelessness, displacement and exile inspired theories of simplistic notions of space and self" and said nothing to "authenticate the agony of uprootedness suffered by Muslims in the last half century" (Majid 2002:11). The September 11 rhetoric brought this point into high relief. We have been conditioned not to have to engage the Other on its own terms. In the weeks following the attack, even the term *Islamism* was absent from discussion. There was a political reason for this: the U.S. government was still toying with coalition building. However, the academic silence regarding Islamism stemmed from the fact that it was not in line with the feel-good discourse on Islam based on the guilt propagated by multiculturalism and postcolonialism. The enemy had to be terrorism, not Islamism (Freund 2001:12). Orientalist guilt and boutique multiculturalist tolerance had dictated the parameters of the discussion. A rabid polemic by a firebrand Italian journalist and the ensuing clamor, however, brought the issue of Occidentalism into discussion in as glaring a manner as the Sokal hoax had done with postmodernism.

THE FALLACI AFFAIR

This challenge to the discourse of Occidentalism appeared in a notorious article by Oriana Fallaci. Best known for her sensational style of reporting in the 1970s, Fallaci lived for twenty years preceeding her death in 2006 in New York City. She was asked by the director of *Corriere della Sera* to describe her reactions to September 11. She responded with a philippic[7] against Islamist terrorism and leveled accusations against Western elites, foremost among them journalists, whose cowardice she felt had contributed to its development. The article, entitled "La Rabbia e l'Orgoglio," appeared on 29 September 2001 and was later published in book form by Rizzoli. This article and its subsequent reworking brought to the fore a lively debate that was pointedly absent from all other open discussions regarding the event. From the White House to pulpits across America, Islamist terror was being presented as a perversion of a great faith by an obscurantist fringe group. Fallaci placed the blame directly on the doorstep of Islam.

In the aftermath of September 11, commentators and critics pointedly questioned the lack of a moderate Muslim condemnation of the attacks. While some have claimed that Muslim repudiation of the violence had gone unreported by bias on the part of the Zionist-based media (Caldwell 2002b), many commented on this marked silence. Where were the voices of the true faithful we kept hearing about? Jean-François Revel looked for the condemnation of the attack by the immense numbers of peacefully inclined European Muslims who likewise had kept silent in 1986 and 1995 (Revel 2003:68–70). In *Libération,* Marc Semo noted that, indeed, few voices in the Muslim world have spoken out clearly against Islamist excesses (cited in Caldwell 2002a). Christopher Caldwell, a religion editor of *The Weekly Standard* seconded this concern, asking where the Muslim-American equivalents were to the German Americans who in 1941 had flocked to army recruitment offices to liberate the world from their first cousins. He pointed to the strong ethnic solidarity among Western Muslims.

Fallaci went much farther than these social commentators. She suggested that Islamicist terror was part and parcel of Islam itself. She claimed that Islam was a religion that wanted nothing to do with liberty, justice, democracy, and progress. This message, fundamental to Fallaci's argument, was, however, overshadowed by her more provocative and vicious comments for which she earned at least four antiracist suits.[8] If one can look past her customary melodramatic and, in this instance, racist, rhetoric to follow the argument, her thesis was actually quite radical. Fallaci was claiming that there was no difference between Islam and Islamism. Her invective had, however, created such furor that this central point became secondary. In fact, this thesis has yet to be debated.

While Fallaci's racist invective was histrionic, odious, and puerile, her real offense was in suggesting that there was something in Islam that made even mainstream believers tacitly sympathetic to Islamist violence. Europe's "regime of solicitude toward minorities," she claimed, had left European societies defenseless against a threat to their civilization. Fallaci opined that Islam was at odds with European culture, even though it was the faith of tens of millions of Europeans. She also asserted that Europe refused to acknowledge this fact. Fallaci directed her attack primarily against the intellectuals and journalists whose comments, as those I have cited above, call for Americans to sympathize with the terrorists' motivations. Caldwell has cited her attacks against journalists such as Tiziano Terzoni, the Asia correspondent for *Der Spiegel* and *Corriere della Sera,* who had called upon the world in the aftermath of September 11 to understand the "drama of the Muslim world in its confrontation with modernity," to understand "the role of Islam in anti-globalization ideology." We do not need, according to Terzoni, a coalition against terrorism, but rather the world needs a "coalition against poverty, exploitation and intolerance" (cited in Caldwell 2002a). It is uncanny how such journalistic responses mirror the rhetoric of academic criticism in its dearth of specifics and particularities of the populations involved as well as its redirecting of responsibility to the West's faults rather than placing accountability on the religious extremists involved. Fallaci was calling attention to the hypocrisy of professional antiracist intellectuals.

Although almost universally condemned, Fallaci did receive some support. As Caldwell has noted, Mia Doornaert of the Belgian daily *De Standaard* accused the antiracists who had condemned Fallaci of using a double standard since far worse was written about Jews and Christians in Islamic publications in Western countries and voiced in mosques in the West on a regular basis. She asked why these journals and individuals were not also prosecuted for hate crimes (cited in Caldwell 2002a). Doornaert also cited the media's habit of minimizing Islamist violence. She noted how Belgian social workers avoid meddling in cultural genital mutilation of its citizens who happen to be Belgian-born daughters of immigrants.

In the *Frankfurter Allgemeine Zeitung* (June 2002), Otto Kallscheuer suggested that Fallaci's book should circulate freely. Antiracist censorship and protecting Muslim sensibilities were, in effect, preventing us from seeing how Fallaci had given the wrong answers to a series of right questions. Fallaci had, in effect, challenged the abuse of police power and the European tendency to criminalize racist attitudes that led to a climate of censorship and state-enforced opinion. The courts were putting the power of the state behind a conformism-enforcing pressure inherent in public opinion. Fallaci viewed antiracism laws as a form of intellectual terrorism. She claimed that the European Left was using the Rights of Man as a tool to corrupt their

countries' judicial systems, making it difficult to fight against Islamist terrorism. Alain Finkielkraut noted that while Fallaci went too far and succumbed
to racist temptation, her book could not be reduced to its unacceptable
formulations. He claimed that, in France today, one cannot say anything bad
about Islamists without automatically praising Islam, in much the same way
that Bush prefaced all his comments after September 11 with initial hymns
of praise to Islam (cited in Caldwell 2002a). Caldwell described the proforma
condemnations of the attacks followed by apologias and warning to the West
not to overreact as stemming from an "outraged sense of entitlement" on
the part of Muslims. The Fallaci episode, her polemic, and its reception were
symptomatic of the general failure of the process of theorizing the Other in
the absence of hermeneutical control. The central point to consider is that the
critique came from a journalist not known for her balanced reasoning, and
the ensuing debate took place in the popular press, not the academic sector
that had claimed to have spent the last thirty years learning to deconstruct
the Other.

FINAL BELIEFS

With September 11, everything came together. It inspired meaningless responses
on the part of academics, such as articles on the Disneyfication of Arabs and
how *The Mummy* tells us something informative about Arab-U.S. relations. We
were treated to numerous "readings" of September 11 as a text. These often
consisted of nothing more than academics discussing not September 11 but
how significant their experience of the event was. There was the postcolonial
appropriation of Orientalist essentialisms to express Occidentalist apologias.
Fallaci gave us a noteworthy example of strong, strong multiculturalism in
her polemical response to the boutique multiculturalism that pervaded the
academic discourse.

   The post-September 11 rhetoric followed three tracks. One track consisted
of wholehearted support of the United States with intense criticism of the
Islamic world (Fallaci 2001; Revel 2003). This track is open to the criticism
that it expresses a new Orientalism. The second track, taking the form of an
Occidentalist critique and deconstruction of U.S. policies and actions vis-à-vis
the Islamic world, presents the United States as the author of its own problems
culminating in September 11. Islamic terror is seen as a function, indeed, a
construction of the hegemonic politics of American administrations (Chomsky
2001; Baudrillard 2002). The charge against this critique is that it unfairly
constructs the United States as an evil empire responsible for all manner of
political and social ills in the Arab world (Revel 2003). We can also identify a

third track, those who sometimes refer to themselves as "concerned patriots," who argue for a view of shared responsibility but, at the same time, expand the definition of September 11 victims to include those willing to stand up and accuse American imperialism. The victims are not only those who lost their lives but also the academics who bravely criticize American imperialism and thereby risk being blacklisted or persecuted. Just as colonialism nips at the heels of the postcolonial critic, so too is McCarthyism often seen to breathe down the neck of academics. It is interesting to note that in this script the victimization of the critical patriot is given as much prominence as, if not more than, the critique itself. The very fact that, with a surplus of real victims, any "victimization" of intellectuals is even voiced speaks volumes. The critic's fate and sacrifice must always be prominently noted.

In these pages, I have tried to show how theories and pedagogies of alterity informed this script by shaping an East never held accountable for its sins and a West debilitated by communal guilt. I have also tried to show how the academic discourses of alterity have brought us no closer to understanding the third world: they have not provided us with the information we will need to coexist in the future or a viable framework within which to function in the present. In an age of supposed globalization, where academe has prided itself on opening up canons and engaging the world in a responsible and comprehensive manner, we misunderstand the Other as much as in any previous era of arrogance, obscurantism, or isolationism. Perhaps we never really wanted to understand. Perhaps we only wanted to think about ourselves (or how we perceive ourselves) and pretend to be "engaged." In response to the suggestion that theory's political utility was dubious, Catherine Stimpson noted that literary theorists were terrified of being seen as politically irrelevant.[9] It is this imposition of the Self into the critical enterprise that distinguishes recent political claims of literary theory from its earlier ideological use. Earlier political readings served a larger social (imperial?) project, whereas the politics now pertain to the individual and are directed primarily at personal glorification rather than the aggrandizement of some larger cause. Shortly after September 11, Derrida was awarded the Theodor Adorno Award and took this occasion to comment on the event. "My unconditional compassion, addressed to the victims of September 11, does not prevent me from saying aloud, with regard to the crime, I do not believe that anyone is politically guiltless" (cited in Žižek 2002:57). What Žižek finds noteworthy here is something that I have tried to show throughout this volume: the self-relating, inclusion of one's Self in the picture. This position of the Self becomes the only true "infinite justice." And the Other? Well, we sympathize with our Muslim brethren, even if we still do not know anything about them.

The pedagogies of alterity have given us nothing but the gestures to use to support this self-fashioning. But the argument can then be made that, with regard to real victimization and minority status, academe has played in the realm of the gestural for a long time. Symbolism supercedes reality. What is important is not inclusion but gestures and perceptions, along with some accompanying sense of self-satisfaction at perceiving oneself to be inclusive.

CHAPTER 7

GESTURES OF INCLUSION

INTRODUCTION

Even before the debris was cleaned up from the two towers and the other fallen buildings, New Yorkers began discussing the types of memorials that might be erected on the site. The New York Fire Department wanted to build a memorial monument similar to the one depicting the soldiers raising the American flag over Iwo Jima. Before the casting of such a statue began, however, there was some concern that the ethnicity of the firemen actually involved in the raising of the flag at the World Trade Center site should be changed. As you may remember, on the day after the bombing, three white firemen raised a flag from one of the fire trucks onto the steel frame that was still standing. This event was caught by photographers and became part of the iconography of the disaster. Rather than show those actual firemen, there were some who thought that the men in the memorial monument should be represented as black, white, and Hispanic figures. Others thought that the statue should depict the actual reality of the situation, rather than some public relations version. The thought was that a racially diverse monument would present the inclusiveness and proportionality that did not and still does not exist. Of the 343 martyred firemen, twenty-four were minority members. It was one thing to represent diversity in recruitment brochures and posters, quite another thing to misrepresent the fidelity of the moment.

It is quite interesting that this debate even took place. As Diana Schaub noted, under our current ideological disposition, color must be seen. If a rainbow is not there, it must be added (Schaub 2002:7). The argument of artistic license is not a valid justification for altering the racial composition of the statues. This idea stemmed from a purely political, rather than aesthetic, judgment. Those who retouched the photo of the event will claim to act out of a desire to pay homage to those black and Hispanic firefighters who died.

In that sense, race can be a relevant category if the purpose of the memorial was to honor the dead, not to depict them. If the argument is that the firemen represent a brotherhood, it should not matter the race of those honored, since they are brothers. In fact, it would suggest segregation not integration, if black men had acted in order to honor fallen black firefighters. The most offense was taken from the notion that something was wrong with the event as it transpired; it needed to be airbrushed (Schaub 2002:8). Clarence Page of the *Chicago Tribune* noted that a multicultural memorial would, in fact, mask patterns of discrimination that fire departments have practiced for decades. It was not accidental that any fire department photo would be monochromatic. Such evidence should stand as "exhibit A" in a court of racial opinion (cited in Schaub 2002:8). An interesting parallel can be drawn between this attempted gesture and the impulses behind multiculturalism and postcolonialism. Both represent a form of politicized inclusion. Both the proposed statue and the efforts made within academe seek to project an image of diversity that is not supported by the numbers.

The underrepresentation of minorities in traditional fields and their balkanization into ethnic studies bear witness to a similar desire on the part of academe to manage minority contributions rather than seek true parity. When affirmative action was adopted a generation ago, it was seen by many as a violation of the fundamental principle of color blindness. It was justified as a temporary expedient to revise the effects of discrimination and exclusion, a necessary evil, desirable under the present circumstances, but not in and of itself. However, privilege and preference, once they are established, are not readily relinquished. To make preferential policies permanent, a new rationale was needed. The call for diversity, which makes race consciousness a positive good, was adopted. Diversity dismissed the old standard of color blindness, declaring it not only impossible but also undesirable (Schaub 2002:13).

As this episode at the World Trade Center and many others[1] show, academic theories of the Other have filtered down into general discourse. Throughout this volume, we have examined the process of cross-fertilization, how theory has informed curricular and institutional initiatives in diversity, and how the marketing needs of institutions have, in turn, influenced theoretical trends. In this final chapter, I would now like to investigate how pedagogies and theories of alterity relate to institutional policies for recruitment. There is a myth of affirmative action that is belied by the statistical evidence. It is my contention that the various theories of alterity examined in this volume provide a master narrative to support this myth. Theoretical constructions of the Other have proliferated in direct proportion to the failure of statistical evidence to support the success claims of affirmative action. In other words, redefinitions of Otherness become necessary lest the continued marginalization and containment of America's minorities within academe under affirmative action be unmasked and revealed. Given this volume's focus on postcolonial theory, I will examine institutional and governmental gestures of inclusion in India and the United States. India, with the longest history of preferences and quotas in the world today, provides an excellent case study in the effectiveness of positive discrimination or affirmative action.

POSITIVE DISCRIMINATION IN INDIA

In 1932, the British created a special electorate for untouchables in India. This instance of preferential treatment for outcastes posed significant problems for Gandhi and the Congress Party. The fear was that untouchables, given a separate voting voice, would not vote in block with their Hindu coreligionists who denied them basic human rights. Gandhi's fear of losing the untouchable vote prompted him to threaten to fast until death in order to prevent the untouchables from gaining the separate electorate. This threatened fast is usually presented in hagiographic terms: Gandhi risked his life in a fast against untouchability. In actuality, it was a cynical strategic ploy on his part to blackmail untouchables into staying within the Hindu fold and delivering votes in favor of a religion that did not grant them any dignity, let alone basic needs (Figueira 2002:150–59). The great untouchable reformer, B. R. Ambedkar, the Columbia University–trained framer of the Indian Constitution, had to accede to Gandhi's ploy, lest the "Mahatma" actually die in this stunt and thereby precipitate a whole-scale massacre of untouchables throughout India. The untouchables were thus prevented from splintering the Hindu vote. At this time, however, they did receive some preferential access to government jobs. Moreover, since the Congress Party and Hindu nationalists had effectively shown their cards, provisions were built into the Indian Constitution to limit the continued exploitation of untouchables after independence. Group preferences of the disadvantaged were stipulated in the Fourteenth Amendment to the Indian Constitution, mirroring the Fourteenth Amendment of the United States Constitution. Those provisions that Ambedkar was able, after much maneuvering, to include in the Constitution established reservations that were intended to forestall political opposition and conflict at the time of independence. They were intended to last for five to ten years and then be cut off. The reservations of 1947, however, are still in place today and are continuously renewed. If they are still on the books, they either have been only partially successful or serve some other purpose. Caste in India, like racial discrimination in the United States, is remarkably resilient.

These provisions were initially intended for untouchables and tribals with severe social disabilities. However, as they were framed, they included an omnibus category of reservations for "other backward classes." Because of this wording, there has occurred in the sixty years since independence a proliferation of preferred groups in India. The original reservations meant for the untouchables and disadvantaged tribal groups were necessary because these groups were outside the caste system and subject to gross inequities. But the miscellaneous classification has come to be used by many individuals and groups within the caste system. In fact, under this omnibus categorization, many more individuals have received preferred treatment than has ever been provided to untouchables and tribals for whom the preferences were created. These "other" deemed backward individuals and groups outnumber the untouchables and, because of their educational, social, and economic standing, they have been in a better position to take advantage of preferences and quotas for government jobs and university admissions. The untouchables, also known as the scheduled castes and the Dalits, comprise 16 percent of the population. Backward tribals make up 8 percent of the population. The "other backward" groups that have arisen in the last thirty years comprise an unbelievable 52 percent of the population (Sowell 2004:24). The provision for "other" disadvantaged groups and individuals has been brilliantly exploited.

Among the other disadvantaged are grouped what we might call the "privileged underprivileged," such as the Chamars of Maharashtra who, although they make up 17 percent of the population, comprise 35 percent of its medical students. Chamars can be middle class, but because of the work they do with leather, they are excluded from caste Hinduism. In Haryana, the Chamars received 65 percent of the graduate-level scholarships and 80 percent of the undergraduate scholarships earmarked for untouchables, according to the *Report of the Commission for Scheduled Castes and Scheduled Tribes* (India 1980:188). The Chamars in Maharashtra have completely monopolized the Dalit quota. These and other "privileged underprivileged" are able to secure reserved places because they are able to fund out of pocket the incidentals that go along with a free education, such as books and supplies, housing, and boarding. These families are in an economic position to absorb the lost labor on farms or lost income. The result is that, as in the United States and elsewhere, the relatively more prosperous tend to enjoy the lion's share of benefits earmarked for the disadvantaged poor.

Also included within the ranks of the "other disadvantaged" are those who represent local preferences. These individuals can be members of groups whom their state favors as less productive natives competing for jobs against more qualified and industrious outsiders who have moved in from other states and thrived. An example of this phenomenon can be seen among the Andhras and the Telanganans. The Andhras had lived under British rule and were advanced in agriculture, education, and general modernization over the Telanganans who had lived under princely rule in Hyderabad and, after independence, found themselves consistently bested on their own turf, despite "safeguards" that had been enforced to protect them. Local preferences speak to such intergroup conflicts.

Other instances of local preference can be seen among the Assamese, who are often surpassed as a group in their own region by more qualified Bengalis and the Marathis of Maharashtra. The Shiv Sena, a grass-roots militaristic group molded on the model of the *Hitlerjugend* and very active in present-day politics of Maharashtra, built its recent strength on polarizing the indigenous Marathis, who barely form a majority, and other ethnic (such as the Gujarati businessmen of Mumbai)[2] and religious groups (such as the Muslims). The Shiv Sena was able to mobilize xenophobic resentment so effectively that it was instrumental in putting the Hindu nationalist BJP Party in charge of the country until its recent upset. Much of the widespread carnage in 1993–94 against the Muslim population instigated by the Shiv Sena and the BJP was explained (and justified) by the deep sense of aggrievement Maharashtrians felt on account of perceived discrimination against them and governmental indulgences supposedly showered on the Muslim minority.

The Shiv Sena's activities in Maharashtra point to another significant factor. Whatever minimal benefits a given segment of the population receives are usually balanced by maximum resentment and hostility. In India today, there is tremendous resentment against the scheduled castes for the places that have been reserved for them even though few actually profit from these reservations. It is not a rare occurrence for people to die in riots over places reserved for untouchables (Joshi 1982:680–82). One can draw a direct correlation between frustration on the part of the "haves" who are not competitive when judged on equal terms and the violence against the "have nots." In the early 1980s, thirteen thousand cases of violent acts committed against untouchables per year were reported, rising in 1986 to sixteen thousand cases, and in the 1990s to twenty thousand cases (Sowell 2004:26). By the late 1990s, the quota system for the backward caste preferences had eliminated whatever good will the upper castes might have been able to muster for the lower castes. Violence against untouchables is directly proportionate to preferential policies even though only 6 percent of untouchable families have in any way benefited from these policies (Ghosh 1996:159–60).

In higher education, most untouchables and members of backward tribes are unable to use the quotas set aside for them and the preferences for which they are entitled. Many spots remain unfilled. When filled, they are disproportionately held by more fortunate members of unfortunate groups. Those spots that are filled by backward classes are situated in less prestigious institutions and in easier and less remunerative fields where students take longer to graduate and there is a big dropout rate (Sowell 2004:30). In 1997, none of the elite universities and engineering institutions had filled their quotas for scheduled castes (Ghosh 1996). The increase in resentment has been accompanied by a proliferation of groups demanding preferential status. In 2001, there were rallies in Rajasthan protesting the inclusion of new groups among the backward classes, asking for separate fixed quotas for the original backward classes so that "new" entrants would not reduce the existing benefits. This effort was essentially an attempt to institute quotas within quotas (Sebastian 2001). In 2007, the Gujjars of Rajasthan took to the streets in violent protest, clamoring for the right to be considered more "backward" than their current classification as an "other backward class." They clashed with the Minas, who opposed their sharing the spoils of tribal backwardness. How "backward" a given group actually is remains open to speculation (Sengupta 2007). In June 2008, the Gujjars succeeded in downgrading their place in the Indian caste system in order to make it easier for them to qualify for reserved government jobs and university quotas (*New York Times* 2008).

The sad reality is that everyone wants and feels they deserve to be a minority. They seek means to minoritize themselves and partake of the benefits presumably squandered on the less fortunate. People who were not born untouchable have worked the system so that they currently hold the majority of seats set aside for untouchables in the legislature. One particularly effective strategy has been for nonuntouchables to gain untouchable status through adoption. This ploy has been particularly successful in Indian academe. While Americans can self-identify as minorities in order to gain access to minority positions in U.S. universities and colleges, in the Indian scenario, high-caste Hindus pay untouchable families for their names so that they can qualify for positions set aside for the scheduled classes. While the American who falsely identifies him/herself as a minority is primarily dishonest, the caste Hindu who gets adopted is both dishonest and exploitative of the untouchables' poverty and peonage. It is fairly common for brahmin students who cannot place into institutions to temporarily become untouchable for entrance into universities and professional schools such as engineering and medicine. They redesignate themselves to take advantage of group preferences and quotas (Galanter 1984:338). These adoptees have found the loophole in the system, one that exists, I believe, in all affirmative action initiatives. What is important to each system is not the number of disenfranchised who actually benefit from such programs as much as the mere fact that there are people filling the spots allotted to the disadvantaged in these institutions. It is crucial to produce a body count, whether or not it actually reflects the population it pretends to represent. It is not necessary for these students to hold anything more than a tenuous position in these institutions of higher learning, nor is it necessary for them to graduate. The point is to produce a make-believe equality. This same cynicism informs affirmative action, as it is currently practiced in the United States.

AFFIRMATIVE ACTION IN THE UNITED STATES

Since both the U.S. Constitution and statutes such as the Civil Rights Act of 1964 stipulate equal rights for individuals, the idea of mandated preferences had to be packaged in America as policies in agreement with the law. Affirmative action, therefore, functions either as a correction of historical inequities or as a policy that encourages diversity and, consequently, a common goal of democratic society. In the United States, affirmative action was initially intended to benefit blacks who were deemed disadvantaged due to their earlier enslavement and subsequent history of maltreatment. As in the case of positive discrimination in India, affirmative action in America has expanded far beyond its initial target population. Unlike India, where social structure is minutely delineated and documented, minority status in America is a more subjective concept and, as such, clouds the extent to which blacks have been eclipsed in the process of affirmative action. Quite simply, the overall effectiveness of affirmative action in America is not as well documented as in India because of our more fluid conception of race and color.[3]

The master narrative of affirmative action's efficacy has influenced how the numbers are tabulated and read. For example, the much-touted 1998 report by William Bowen (former president of Princeton) and Derek Bok (former president of Harvard) affirms the success of affirmative action for blacks admitted to elite institutions with lower qualifications (Bowen and Bok 1998). Their conclusions differ significantly from other similar studies. What is left out of their statistical documentation is the fact that they submerged the blacks admitted under lower standards with the pool of blacks admitted under the same standards as the whites admitted (Sowell 2004:152–54). In this instance, the statistics have been cooked to provide the script needed to confirm affirmative action's success.

However, in his comparative analysis of affirmative action initiatives throughout the world, Thomas Sowell has shown that the American statistical data provides a glaringly different picture for those who choose to read it in a historical perspective. Sowell shows how between 1940 and 1970 the education levels of blacks rose to almost parity with their white counterparts. In 1940, black men on an average attained levels of 5.4 years of education as opposed to white men who attained 8.7 years. By 1970, however, black men had almost reached levels of parity with their white counterparts with 12.1 years of education compared to the 12.7 years average for white men. This rise in the education levels of black men had risen proportionately to black economic growth. In 1940, 87 percent of black families in America lived below the poverty level as opposed to the 47 percent of blacks living in poverty in 1960. This economic growth of an astounding 40 percent took place before the enactment of civil rights legislation and paralleled the exodus of some 3 million blacks from the South and its substandard schools. By 1970, 30 percent of black families lived below the poverty line. During the decade of the enactment of federal affirmative action policies, the poverty of black families dropped by 1 percent to 29 percent (Sowell 2004:118–19). Affirmative action did not improve the economic and educational situation of blacks in America; blacks themselves did, by dint of hard work and perseverance in a discriminatory environment (Thernstrom and Thernstrom 1997:189–94).

As in the case of India, affirmative action was a boon to the fortunate, as any analysis of the minority beneficiaries of government contracts show. Between 1967 and 1992, the top 20 percent of black income earners rose at the same rate as the top 20 percent of white income earners. However, the bottom 20 percent of black income earners saw their income share fall at double the rate of the bottom 20 percent of white income earners (Sowell 2004:120). The reason for this loss of ground among poor blacks can be attributed to the fact that immigrants are eligible for the same affirmative action benefits as blacks, even though they themselves have not suffered past discrimination in the United States (Sowell 2004:121). The majority of government contracts for "minority-owned" businesses from 1986–90 went to European businessmen from Portugal. Minority businesses rent out their minority status. While they are ostensibly owned by blacks, they serve as fronts for and benefit whites. Asian entrepreneurs immigrating to the United States receive a large portion of the preferential access to government contracts (Sowell 2004:121). These figures suggest that, in the last two decades, the reality of affirmative action benefits is at radical odds with its rationale. What was intended to benefit blacks benefits four times as many businesses owned by Hispanics and Asian Americans and thirteen times as many businesses owned by women (Ibid.). Similarly, in education, the advantage of being black has declined sharply between 1972–92 in first-tier colleges. In the 1970s, blacks with a given set of test scores and grades had a 13% greater likelihood of being admitted to these schools. That bonus dropped to a 5% greater likelihood in the 1990s

(Brewer 1999, cited in Brown, Carnoy, and Currey, et al. 2003:114). The reason for this shift is obvious. As in India, affirmative action has been extended in the United States to include groups that were not initially considered in the Civil Rights Act of 1964. This extension was possible due to the definition of the term *discrimination* by the act to mean intentional actions by an employer against individuals as distinguished from disparate consequences of particular tests or other criteria on different groups.

The single most significant reason that American blacks do not benefit more from affirmative action is that "being disenfranchised" has been extended to new groups that have not suffered anything close to the social disadvantages that blacks have suffered in America. This process consists of opportunity hoarding by one group to the detriment of another (Brown, Carnoy, and Currey, et al. 2003:191). The largest group to benefit from affirmative action in America has been women, and most of these women are white. For white women, the argument in favor of preference cannot be the legacy of slavery. In fact, no specific harm or discrimination is demanded for the beneficiaries of gender preferences, since the statistics would hardly prove such discrimination. Women have benefited from the reconceptualization of affirmative action. In addition to correcting historical inequity, affirmative action now also promotes diversity.

In 1920, women comprised 34 percent of the bachelor degrees and 15 percent of the doctorates awarded in the United States as opposed to 24 percent and 10 percent respectively in 1950. For those same years, female degrees in mathematics declined from 15 percent to 5 percent and degrees in engineering from 10 percent to 2 percent. As opposed to the situation of blacks, in the latter half of the twentieth century, the education level (degrees awarded) and job rate declined for women. Throughout the 1950s and 1960s, there was not one year when there were as many masters and doctorates for women as there were in the 1930s. Over this time period, either the male power structure was becoming more discriminatory against women as the twentieth century progressed or a favorable economic climate increased the birth rate that, in turn, decreased the number of women gaining advanced degrees. The statistics do show that female education is directly tied to birth rates. Between 1940 and 1950, the baby boom years, they decreased by 9 percent. The year of 1902 showed education/job rates doubling that of 1958 (Johnson 1980:51). As the birth rate declined in the 1960s, female representation in jobs and education rose proportionately (Sowell 2004:13–35).

Just as in the case of women, the new groups who benefit from the expanded pool of preferences, such as immigrants from Latin America, Europe, and Asia, cannot lay claim to the "legacy of slavery" argument to justify why they should receive preferences instead of blacks (Sowell 2004:136). As in the case of blacks, the "lingering effects" of oppression do not really hold for women, since they feasibly are able to share in the social benefits that their fathers, grandfathers, and male ancestors have accrued. In 1970, blacks comprised two-thirds of the individuals who were entitled to affirmative action; by the year 2000, they made up 49 percent of those who enjoyed its preferences (Sowell 2004:137). Whatever benefits black men have acquired relative to those enjoyed regularly by white men are more than outweighed by the disadvantages they experience in relation to those received by white women.

The history of affirmative action in America is one that showcases the supposed benefits it has bestowed upon blacks, while essentially serving the needs of and "positively discriminating" in favor of Latin Americans, Europeans, Asians, and white women. In fact, one can argue that affirmative action has even contributed to an increased failure rate of blacks due to the effect of race norming[4] and pervasive shifting, the mismatching of minority students with institutions that serve the institutional demographics more than the students in question. The overwhelming demand for increased minority "body counts" in all educational institutions has set up a double standard of achievement in which administrators and faculty collude. Minority students who can be successful in any number of settings are turned into failures by mismatching them by preference in admissions, not holding them to competitive standards and balkanizing them into courses of study that are less competitive, where they can even partake of affirmative grading policies.[5]

Balkanizing minorities into less rigorous ethnic studies departments, grade inflation for such programs, and reducing the failure rate to validate these ethnic studies programs' continued existence all contribute to the continued marginalization of minorities. What becomes quickly apparent is that the need for numbers of people of color is all that matters. It does not correspond to the number of those credentialed through shifting and their subsequent failure to thrive in an educational environment, where they are nothing more than a number on some administrator's spreadsheet of success in diversity.

In 1995, to great hue and cry, the legislature of California banned racial preferences and quotas in institutions of higher education in their state. In 1996, Texas followed suit. As predicted, black enrollment in the flagship schools of the system, Berkeley and Austin, declined. The general enrollment throughout the system, however, rose. Once preferences were banned, students were no longer encouraged to shift to institutions for the sake of the institution's demographics rather than the students' tested skill level. In essence, blacks redistributed themselves. The ensuing clamor centered on how minority enrollments in the flagship campuses were down rather than on how many more students, in the wake of the banning of preferences, graduated. Whether their success rates have increased is less important than the cosmetic loss to the institutions in question.

COSMETIC ENHANCEMENT

The system as it is presently constructed and the way in which it functions makes it attractive to be minoritized and labeled "disadvantaged." The theories of the margin examined in this volume are constructed precisely to aid in this process of autominoritization. They are constructed to redefine what it is to be disadvantaged, and these redefinitions are subsequently incorporated into university policies of diversity. The process shows a clear disregard for the relativity of suffering. The system has been constructed in such a way that it can be easily exploited by individuals who are not particularly disadvantaged—privileged white females, well-to-do Latin Americans, whites with an infinitesimal percentage of American-Indian blood in their veins[6] and elites from the third world. This process works particularly well for "postcolonial subjects" who come from cultures already presented as disadvantaged because of colonialism. They slide easily into American society where a premium is placed on setting aside disadvantage. Quite simply, it is easy to make room for model minorities who can be defined as disadvantaged but are actually as educated, entitled, and elitist as those holding the reins of power. They have the "right face" for the establishment. In the case of Indian postcolonials, with decades of experience manipulating a preferential system and caste privilege, the transition is seamless.

On an intellectual level, the theories of migrancy we have examined in these pages are questionable, especially the gimmickry of metaphorical exile, hybridity, and marginalization. On a practical level, however, they are brilliantly conceived and deeply meaningful in light of American affirmative action policy. What we witness in these various theories of alterity is not just bad taste or a rarefied intellectual game devoid of reality. In light of affirmative action, they become the intellectual capital to reinforce a position that individuals and institutions want to maintain. These pedagogies of alterity present a culturally acceptable and sophisticated form of racism, since they leave the institutional benefits of being "othered" invisible and untouched. Why would an upper-class Indian professor at an elite institution stand in front of a room full of white people and claim that his experience is the same as that of ghetto blacks. Such gestures are not just misinformed or perverse. In terms of how preferences work in both India and the United States, such a claim makes sense as a tried and true means of positioning the self, appropriating an identity, and receiving advantages in a labor market that substantially disadvantages blacks and Hispanics. Without the "smoking gun" of intentionality, one cannot be deemed to discriminate in terms of race (Brown, Carnoy, and Currey, et al. 2003:58). There is also a double cachet: the personal and the intellectual group both benefit. One can exhibit contempt for former Western colonial power and be compensated for doing so.

On an institutional level, the South Asian phenomena described in these pages betoken a wider problem with the development from identity politics to identity hiring and institutional task assignment, which leads to that most pernicious manifestation in which knowledge becomes both a group preoccupation and a group possession. An African American student knows intuitively that Latin literature is his heritage (as much as anyone); a Bengali girl knows that she can have a career in classics; and a Persian boy knows that he knows ancient history. Yet the authorization of identity voiced in postmodernism withholds its certification. In the end, it all appears to be another facet of neoracism, the essential doctrine of which is that the *politēs/civis* does not autonomously fashion his/her cultural *persona* but must play out a script assigned to him/her by some overarching authority (in practice, for our argument, a university administration).

The reality is that before multiculturalism and postcolonialism, there should have been the needed decolonization of the Other in the United States (Guerrero 1996:49). Without this decolonization, multiculturalism and postcolonialism as academic dogmas and orthodoxies function as disciplinary and "institutionalized apartheid" (Guerrero 1996:50). Minority scholars realize very quickly that their success is tied to being a "professional minority"—a minority doing the minority thing or performing as a dancing bear. Initially aided by the system, these minority scholars are subsequently exploited and neutralized by the system. Minorities who do not fit the profile (i.e., who do not specialize in topics reflecting their ethnicity or gender) are certainly "in the minority." Moreover, their institutional value is limited since their cosmetic purpose (a visible minority showcasing an institution's commitment to minority studies) is reduced by half.[7] Postcolonialism and multiculturalism are, indeed, strategies of containment and cooptation.

It is curious to note that in many institutions, the minority hire is called a "target of opportunity" position. This nomenclature is quite revealing. The military term *target of opportunity* generally refers to secondary targets only scoped once the real target is inaccessible or has been missed. Even in naming minority positions and publicizing them, institutions distinguish "what is preferable" and what is to be attained by default. Calling minorities "targets of opportunity" suggests that "real" hires are inaccessible (funding, quotas), and a minority is hired by default.[8] Theory feeds this process by presenting the nonethnic with accommodationist resolutions. With all the theories studied in these pages, Euro-American privilege remains intact. In fact, the manner in which the Other is taught supports belief in as well as the presumed superiority of Western civilization. Theories of alterity have not allowed raced groups to move beyond the show and tell domestication of late-nineteenth-century folklore (Cruz 1996:32). The Other remains an externally imposed exotic caricature transformed into a cultural text.

The Collecting of the Other

Je suis un étranger ici, un Indien en exil.

—Paul Gauguin, *Correspondence de Paul Gauguin*

In "L'essai sur l'exotisme" (1904), Victor Segalen placed the exotic exclusively in the realm of the real and authentic as an unmediated response to the impenetrable Other. However, the exotic event also results in an incomplete hermeneutic circle. While the Other is grasped, it is never assimilated. The encounter with the Other that foregrounds the exotic project is thus foreclosed. In Segalen's estimation, we simply cannot make the Other our own. It remains, on its deepest level, inaccessible and incapable of appropriation or comprehension,[1] even if we continually make efforts to do so. Segalen may very well have been correct in his evaluation. Nevertheless, two strategies have historically been employed to bridge the gap of (in)accessibility to the exotic—strategies that Segalen himself did not shy away from practicing. The two methods devised to attempt to capture the exotic involve the souvenir and the art of collecting.

The souvenir and the collectable are closely linked but radically different assemblages of objects. Both are evocations of the past with different aesthetics. The souvenir focuses on origin and presence, restoration and provenance. The collection deals with accumulation and exchange. The souvenir speaks through a language of longing. Collecting, in contrast, is a process of retrieval and ordering of things past (Stewart 1993:135). In these concluding remarks, I would like to relate the theories and pedagogies of alterity examined in this volume to these two aesthetics. I see the commodification of alterity in recent theory and pedagogy as conforming to an aesthetics of collecting or acquisition. Both exhibit a need to retrieve and order. However, this Other, once retrieved, also functions as a souvenir, since it is intended for use as a commodity to be bartered and exchanged. Its acquisition satisfies the nostalgic longing to preserve the gestures and fictions of inclusion or acculturation that institutions labor to create and the engagement or insight that individual intellectuals devote considerable effort to elaborate and sustain. Collected objects exert power over their collectors. Walter Benjamin, an avid collector himself, viewed collecting as an attempt to forge an intimate relationship with objects in order for the collector to come alive and live more fully through them.[2] Collecting the Other serves a function of self-fashioning and self-validation, whether the collector is a hobbyist or an academic professional.[3]

   The Other, like the collected object, is ideal. They both reflect images not of what is real but of what is desired. The collected object is a mirror constructed so as to throw back a desirable image of the Self (Rheims 1959:50). This will to power is clearly evident in a colonial collector, such as Segalen. It betokens a form of collecting that the anthropologist James Clifford has qualified as typically "Western"—collecting as a strategy for the deployment of a possessive Self, culture, and authenticity (Bal 1994:104). The quest for authenticity is at the heart of collecting. Souvenirs have a capacity to serve as traces of authentic experience (Stewart 1993:135). One does not need souvenirs of events that are repeatable. Rather, one seeks out souvenirs of events whose materiality has escaped us, events that exist only through the invention of narrative, the "second-hand" experience of its possessor. The narrative of the object is a narrative of authenticity. It is also a narrative of the possessor.[4] It serves to authenticate a past or otherwise removed experience (Stewart 1993:135). In the case of the pedagogies under investigation, the Other is not the third-world "native" whose incomprehensibility and impenetrability Segalen established in the "Essai sur l'exotisme" and whose customs and race he did not pretend to assimilate. The world literary text as souvenir represents and authenticates the academic construction of the exotic Other. It was through the text as souvenir of the Other that critics seek, in Benjamin's terminology, to "come alive" or, in Baudrillard's formulation, to eroticize their own being (Baudrillard 1994:19). They are the props with which academics authenticate a myth of the artist, a myth in which they also participate, both as artists and collectors.

   Collecting the Other and creating narratives enable critics to rehabilitate themselves and share in the Other's singularity and significance. The appropriation of the cultural production of the third world attests to the critic's double role as a collector and author. As a collector, critics can traffic these culturally othered artifacts as exotic products, characterized not by their remoteness but by their proximity and availability in an English department. Third-world literature becomes authentic only through cultural dislocation, as when "native" art exists because it is exhibited in Western households (Appadurai 1986:28). The collected object has meaning, therefore, only in relation to the collecting subject. Collecting is a process, according to Elsner and Cardinal, whereby one becomes conscious of oneself. Collecting is a gesture of nostalgia for previous/other worlds with an added level of amusement and caprice (Elsner and Cardinal 1994:5). After all, collecting concerns itself with the accumulation of such things as shells (even in an otherwise serious person as Neruda), key rings, and matchboxes. What is important to note is that the collector of matchboxes or the multiculturalist specialist consumes the landscapes of these places. Collecting is by nature imperialistic.

Rajini Srikanth has drawn this connection between the hegemonizing nature of collecting and multiculturalism as a new form of imperialism, particularly in the field of publishing. In Europe, 40 to 50 percent of the books published and sold in bookstores are translations. In the United States, only 3 percent of the books published are translations (Salamon 2004; cited in Srikanth n.d.:1). These statistics speak volumes for the provincialism, cultural arrogance, and general ignorance of the American reading public. In response to this phenomenon, a group of concerned scholars have established an online magazine for international literature entitled *Words without Borders*[5] that collects representative literature from around the world labeled in the following fashion: Africa/Americas/ Asia/Europe/Middle East/ Pacific Rim Cities/ Coasts/Mountains/Plains/Deserts/Forests/Villages. What is significant here is the manner in which this initiative to be multicultural configures the world, portioning it as cartographical units, not as real places.[6] This way of viewing the world speaks volumes for how multiculturalism has devised a hegemonic, leveled out, and intellectually meaningless construction of alterity.

Multiculturalism claims to redistribute rights and radically rethink issues of recognition when, in fact, it does nothing but fetishize knowledge and create a smokescreen for societal and institutional unwillingness to change the academic situation of minorities. Theory and pedagogy avoid grappling with race and difference under the pretense of doing something, as in the above noted Internet initiative. Like *Words without Borders,* multiculturalism exhibits an inferential racism when it breeds and encourages ethnicity-oriented scholarship that contributes to the continued marginalization of minorities within academe. As we have shown, multiculturalism works against affirmative action, by feigning an institutional commitment to minority hiring where little, in fact, exists, especially in those institutions where nonminorities assume the role of minorities with administrative blessings. Strategies of containment obscure power and privilege rather than redistribute rights and rethink recognition. Even with multiculturalism and postcolonialism firmly installed in academic institutions, the standards are still defined, the purpose of the humanities is still articulated, and the manner in which they are articulated (as bland, watered-down versions) are as they always have been. With multiculturalism, ethnicity is used to mask hegemonic domination with the pretext of pluralist tolerance. As in postcolonialism, difference is valorized in order to guarantee sameness. In all the pedagogies of alterity studied in this volume, there is a significant problem of spokespersonship. The critics engage in what has been termed "expressive individualism," where privileged individuals identify with minorities. Theories of the margin have become a central mode for attaining such personal validation. There is no empowerment of the Other here. In reality, the monolingual, white, male scientist dean usually still determines how cultures come together and are taught.

I have presented the theories and pedagogies examined in this volume as responses to affirmative action and its erosion of traditional power bases in both India and America. They provide opportunities to regain perceived lost privileges. They work in conjunction with the disciplinary cooptation of the world by fields without grounding in cultural specificity. By this, I mean, those areas of the globe that were previously studied within the context of linguistic, historical, or philosophical particularity now tend to be studied in English departments, humanities centers, women's studies, and ethnic studies. In the process of such cooptation, the third world has become leveled out and commodified.

The postcolonial critic, like the native informant, uses personal experience to package a structure. The critic takes on a role that is not dissimilar to that of the area studies specialist in the 1950s with regard to the objectified Other who is discursively constructed. Like the area studies specialist serving cold war politics, the postcolonial critic serves diaspora politics. The postcolonial critic also resembles the brahmin who serves as the ideal reader and authoritative critic. Just as the brahmin, so too do these critics of the Other presume to disseminate a vision of national culture and its internal Others. Like brahmins, they too manage the Other through objectifying discourse.

The metaphors of migrancy all pretend to be liberatory and imply an equal mobility where none exists. In the process of theorists speaking for the Other, there is a disquieting tendency to empty words of their pain, as when a term such as *exile* becomes a model for a privileged intellectual who is unusually responsive. The Other serves as fodder for the critic's performance of virtual marginality. Theories of the margin, periphery, and exile allow critics/pedagogues to distance themselves from global capitalism without losing their actual space of comfort. It does not matter that the critics are irreducibly different from the subaltern, since false consciousness has come to dominate so many critical endeavors. Using the third-world Other to valorize the first-world Self becomes a strategy of empowerment and a form of exoticism. The exotic escape from bourgeois values found in the theories of alterity reach their acme, perhaps, in the figure of the nomad. Whereas the multicultural or postcolonial subjects can relate to real individuals, the theoretical nomad reflects nothing real. All these heterologies announce the absolute failure of theory and pedagogy to deal with the Other, a point that was brought into sharp relief on September 11 by the manner in which the events of the day were deconstructed. An odd challenge to the Occidentalist readings of September 11 came from an unexpected source, a journalistic tirade and the debate that it engendered. Even before September 11, however, critics such as Said, Spivak, and Derrida had revealed a need to reevaluate.

In the *MLA Newsletter,* Edward Said called for a return to the classical protocols of critical thinking (plausible interpretation, systemic analysis, adequate contextual support) and to the Western canon (Said 1999:3). Said's statement is curious since he himself never actually ever left the Western canon (although his work indicted those who had inaccurately endeavored to do so), and his concept of Orientalism spawned an entire school of criticism that eschewed this very methodology. The critique of Orientalism (along with its avatars, postcolonialism, and its domestication in the form of multiculturalism), in fact, bears some responsibility for the manner in which literature is being taught in schools and universities today. Yet it seems that while partially responsible for the trend sanctioning such readings, Said was decrying by the end of the 1990s the harmful effects of recent theories on literature. "All manner of frag-mented, jargonized subjects of discussion now flourish in an ahistorical limbo" (Said 1999:3). He saw a reckless abandonment of what could be the common intellectual pursuit in favor of highly specialized, exclusivist, and rebarbative approaches that destroy and undercut the historical as well as social basis of the humanities. Said pleaded for a return to historical analysis, requiring ideas be put into logical relation and overall perspective. Said also cast doubt on involving the study of literature in "a sociopolitical struggle over such issues as identity, gender difference, postcolonial politics and theoretical innovation for its own sake," especially if they led away from the teaching of canonical works (Said 1999:3). He asked his colleagues to abandon exclusivist approaches for the sake of commonality. He was essentially calling for a return to a Gada-merian dialogue (Rapaport 2001:156). Had Said, like Spivak, undergone some conversion process? When Said asked for a return to the Western canon and hermeneutical inquiry was his appeal merely a form of false consciousness? Those very methods to which he now encouraged us to return, his career-making work had earlier encouraged us to abandon. It appears that disciplinary roots and curricular coherence were once again in vogue.

It was truly astonishing when Derrida, like Said and Spivak, also asked for a return to theoretical origins of literary analysis. Derrida employed the classical protocols of hermeneutical inquiry (attention to history, content, philology, structure, logic, and agreement) as the primary lines of defense at the moment he sensed that deconstruction had been maligned, as in his response (Derrida 1999:223) to Spivak's attack in "Ghostwriting" (Spivak 1995). Although Derrida had decades earlier launched a critique of Gadamer's hermeneutical conception of interpretative agreement (Michelfelder and Palmer 1989), he retreated into the arms of hermeneutical fair play when it suited his cause (Rapaport 2001:xiii). More false consciousness? Perhaps. More likely, there appeared to be a general recognition of a need to return to a Gadamerian dialogue where hermeneutical listening and receptivity become relevant and tradition is viewed as an infinite conversation in which horizons fuse and break open. Perhaps there is even some acknowledgment that institutions have become too compartmentalized and theorists espouse theories that have become insular and degraded in an uncritical, incoherent, and arbitrary morass (Rapaport 2001:88–89).

What seems so apparent in this entire process is that the creation of all these "isms" has served theorists well, making careers for their creators and acolytes at the same time. The poststructuralist revolution wonderfully parallels the structuralist revolution of the 1960s, when theoretical innovation and interdisciplinarity were good for career advancement until the market was glutted and retrenchment called for a retreat from theoretical experimentation and a return to canonical aesthetic values. Self-interest and careerism have consistently dictated the terms of theoretical innovation in the last half-century. Just as the reality effect kicked in after structuralist ideals had degenerated in the mid-1970s, so too the bankruptcy of the theories of alterity and their inconsequentiality caused their staunchest proponents to retreat. They became born-again comparatists. Those who in the past called for revolution, now, at the acme of their brilliant careers, bring an even greater messianic zeal to their new mission. They tell those of us in the trenches, who are exhausted by having spent countless hours trying to decipher their language and logic for undergraduates, "Oops, never mind." Their turnabout suggests the extent to which major proponents of the theories and pedagogies of alterity recognized that "the gig was up" and it was time to shift gears. We can now go back to the methodology of our teachers. The theories of alterity have served us well, having taught us how to be special—a victim and/or a minority. Thanks to theories of alterity, even straightforward Orientalists doing the most culturally chauvinistic study of canonical issues can claim to be in the subject position of an oppressed and marginalized minority (Chow 1993:108–13). The same can be said of scholars studying mainstream canonical authors.

It should be clear that from its structuralist beginnings to post–September 11 sophistries, the theoretical lineage we have traced has become increasingly disengaged from any possibility of praxis in concrete reality. In fact, over the course of time, the definition of praxis itself has been altered to reflect its purely rhetorical function. We have also seen how at various points there was no lack of authoritative critics who questioned the lack of limits, self-referentiality, and ethical blindness of structuralist, poststructuralist, and postmodern theory. Their reservations went largely unheeded. The result has been theory unencumbered by methodological, ethical, psychological, or sociological constraints. The self-promotion, careerism, and conceptual emptiness of multiculturalism and postcolonialism should not surprise us. The fact that the attacks of September 11 and their aftermath exposed the lamentable lack of expertise in and understanding of the contemporary Muslim world underlines how useless in any practical sense this mode 'of theorizing has become.

As I have tried to show in this volume, it is problematic that culturalism, whether it be multiculturalism, postcolonialism, ethnicity studies, or nomadology, has come to define our encounters with otherness, transforming analysis into excessive concern with ethnicity and politics into identity politics. Culturalism has contributed to the undermining of the social on both the national and global level (Dirlik 1997:250). It is this culturalism that needs to be challenged. It has been a central thesis of this volume that culturalism, seen as an indispensable companion of economic new liberalism, seeks to contain genuine difference, which is situational-historical, with pieties about presenting cultural integrity and presents a "fetishistic scientism that privileges generality over specifics" (Dirlik 1997:251). Culturalisms have been appropriated by those making claims to cultural purity in order to assume the prerogatives of speaking for entire societies. These same culturalisms have then been used by elites with their own political agendas to the detriment of those who continue to be disenfranchised.

NOTES

CHAPTER 1

1. My argument throughout this chapter benefited greatly from François Dosse, *Histoire du structuralisme,* originally published in 1991. The references to Dosse, for convenience, refer to the more readily available 1997 English translation of that work, *History of Structuralism.* For those interested in a more detailed discussion of the sources and history here addressed, I refer them to Dosse's work.

2. In particular, structuralism offered a solution to ethnology's image problem. The fact that it had been linked since its inception to colonialism tainted ethnology as a discipline. Structuralist ethnology mitigated this problem. It projected an ideal identity onto external space, providing transcendent models upon which to base a discipline perceived to be compromised. For further discussion, see Raoul and Laura Makarius, *Structuralisme ou Ethnologie* (1973).

3. Oversimplified applications and outright distortions of Kuhn swept through the social sciences and humanities in the 1970s and would continue to thrive well into the nineties culminating in the Sokal hoax, where a physicist revealed how easy it had become to publish extreme scientific absurdities, if they were clothed in the proper literary critical jargon.

4. In particular, see LeRoy Ladurie's *Montaillou, village Occitan de 1294 à 1324* (1975).

5. This allusion refers to Kristeva's novel *Les samouraïs* (1990), which deals with her structuralist adventure and is an obvious homage to Simone de Beauvoir's *Les mandarins* of 1954.

6. Barthes gave himself over to biography in *Roland Barthes par Roland Barthes* (1975) and *Fragments d'un discours amoureux* (1977). In his own journey to the exotic, Barthes visited a Zen monastery in Japan and began spiritual exercises in 1978.

7. One of the last gasps of the gestural life or the ethics of conviction (rather than an ethics of responsibility) can be seen in Foucault's 1978 visit to Iran, where we hear of the liberating nature of the fundamentalist Islamic government as a new incarnation of resistance against oppression.

8. It became known that Paul de Man, an important proponent of deconstruction at Yale, had published collaborationist and anti-Semitic articles in two Belgian papers in

the 1940s. This revelation gave rise to much discussion regarding deconstruction's appraisal of history and subjectivity. To make matters worse, Derrida and some American deconstructionists deconstructed de Man's problematic statements, "interpreting" away the offending passages and denying their evident meaning. What began as a vexing public relations problem became farcical.

9. Rapaport explains this formulation in the following terms: One must not neglect in teaching a modern literature course, to offer a wide distribution of different social perspectives (racial, ethnic, gendered). Any such lack of distribution, can be perceived not just as a failure in accurate representation but as a social act that can be construed as egregiously hostile to social diversity and hence certain constitutencies, "if not all progressive students" (Rapaport 2001:105). Therefore, the course lacking diverse voices not only represents bigotry, the instructor can be labeled a bigot.

CHAPTER 2

1. Southerners have completely fetishized the Civil War; it is not even called the "Civil War," but goes under a number of euphemisms—the War of Secession, the War of Northern Aggression, and so on. Even today, Northerners based in the South are still the enemy. Cars are festooned with bumper stickers announcing "The only good Yankee is a dead Yankee." The Confederate flag, a symbol to Northerners and blacks of the South's glorification of the slave economy, has become a focal point of state defiance and is hung with menacing pride from public and private buildings.

2. The brochure for the Georgia League of the South claims that their organization promotes the "education of our children in the truth." It insists "upon an accurate portrayal of our history and our culture" and prides itself on representing "an honorable people rebuilding a noble society." It wants to see "a return" to the Bible and the Constitution: "We are the fastest-growing grass-roots organization demanding an end to federal tyranny and a return to the principle of States' Rights as guaranteed under the tenth amendment of the Bill of Rights. . . . We seek to advance the cultural, social, economic, and political well-being and independence of the Southern people by all honorable means." The Confederate Society of America solicits new members in reenactor newspapers: "Tired of Yankee Lies? Confederate bashers? Want action instead of talk? We challenge Dixie haters, reverse racists, government pinkos" (*The Civil War Courier* December 2000:52). The Carolina Sutlers sell a bumper sticker announcing that the car owner is a Civil War reenactor and claims that, as such, he is "Keeping History Alive."

3. There is also a long history of reenactments in the North. Northerners reenact the Revolutionary War in addition to the Civil War. Southern reenactments of the Civil War differ from those in the North by their strident efforts to "rewrite" history. The Southern reenactments produce a hobbyist literature that reflects a politics of resentment as a motivating force.

4. See also in this regard, Palumbo-Liu (2002) who sees multiculturalism as a result of the civil rights era. How the language of civil rights (inclusion, equality of representation) has been coopted by multiculturalism has been noted as a negative force (Brennan 1997:115) and a positive one (Giroux 1992).

5. In fact, as David Rieff has argued, the treasured catchphrases of multiculturalism—"cultural diversity," "difference," the need to "do away with boundaries"—resemble the stock phrases of the modern corporation: "product diversification," "the global world," and the "boundary-less company" (Jacoby 1994b:123).

6. As a University of Wisconsin faculty committee expressed it, there is general belief that an ethnocentric view pervades mainstream curriculum and that it "is restricted to the Euro-American experience. Excluded and left invisible are the people of color whose labor and sacrifices have been and continue to be neglected" (San Juan 1995:224). Due to this situation, the committee claimed, American students have been made insensitive to and intolerant of cultural and ethnic difference.

7. In particular, see Joel Kotkin, *Tribes: How Race, Religion and Identity Determine Success in the New Global Economy* (1993); Robert D. Kaplan, *The Ends of the Earth* (1996); and Benjamin R. Barber, *Jihad vs. McWorld: How Globalism and Tribalism Are Reshaping the World* (1995).

8. Huntington divides the world up into a discrete group of civilizations: Sinic, Japanese, Hindu, Islamic, Western, Latin American, and possibly African.

9. In his critique of Huntington, Francis Fukuyama notes that it is not the simplistic clash of civilizations model that we should be investigating, but rather, the clash between modernization and those threatened by modernization and its moral component, human rights (Fukuyama 2001).

10. The Huntington thesis is particularly subversive not because it is ill-conceived, but because it posits multiculturalism as a bane to America's existence and attacks the cultural politics that multiculturalism supports (Palumbo-Liu 2002:118).

11. With the end of the cold war, Palumbo-Liu envisions the need for an opposing Other and he asserts that this role has been assigned to ethnic minorities in the United States. In fact, Palumbo-Liu views any discussion of civilization as dangerous for minority rights (Palumbo-Liu 2002:110).

12. As a politics of identity and recognition, multiculturalism can be traced much further back to the modern concept of 'individual dignity' at the heart of the Enlightenment and bourgeois revolution (Taylor 1994). While identity theorists might embrace a skepticism toward unwarranted universalisms, their revolt rested on the Enlightenment's taste for equality and diversity as well as its objection to arbitrary power (Gitlin 1995:215). Taylor claimed that the politics of difference had its roots in the works of Rousseau and Herder where the individual is seen to have his own measure and universal human rights impose that one tribe's dignity must not infringe on that of another tribe (Taylor 1994:29–30).

13. Fish claims that you do not respond to evil with tolerance, assuming that its energies will dissipate in the face of scorn; you respond to it by stamping it out (Fish 1997:392).

14. The idealized Other of multiculturalism dances fascinating dances and has an ecologically sound holistic approach to reality, while practices such as wife-beating remain out of sight (Žižek 2002:11).

15. The function of spectacle and consumption with regard to multiculturalism has resonance in the Canadian context, where the initiative is institutionally and governmentally widespread. University multicultural initiatives have been compared to the caravans organized each year under Ontario's federal multicultural policy. Each of the varied "cultures" represented in Ontario has its own float and is paraded through the streets "for the WASPS to gaze upon, for the . . . vultures to devour, hence the Quebecois' term 'multivulturalism' " (Davis 1996:45).

16. Gates opposes the thesis of cultural equity, the notion that since people are equal under the law, their productions must therefore be considered as representative of those groups and at least of equal value to other groups (Gates 1992:71).

CHAPTER 3

1. A similar focus on Bengal holds true for the field of Indian studies. Bengali studies has long dominated Western analyses of India. Bengal stands for India as a whole. This situation reflects Bengal's centrality to the consolidation of British colonial power as well as its own sense of itself as the most sophisticated intellectual language, literature, and culture of India. The history of Bengali immigration to the United States has also been significant.

2. The exception to this rule are Ranajit Guha's Subaltern studies historians. The focus on the British imperialism in India stands in contrast to the fact that early theorists of colonialism (such as Fanon, Césaire, Senghor, and Memmi) focused on the French empire.

3. One critic has even placed postcolonialism in virtual space. One cannot judge, we are informed, the validity of postcolonial theory by an existing body of texts because it depends "on a time space of subject formation" (Prashad 2000:58).

4. In this respect, postcolonialism resembles multiculturalism. Both fields of inquiry have difficulty defining themselves. One thinks of the following definition offered by Shohat and Stam (2003:6): "The concept of multiculturalism, then, is above all protean, plural, conjectural, existing in shifting relation to various institutions, discourses, disciplines, communities and nation states. Multiculturalism is a situated utterance, inserted in the social and shaped by history. It can be top-down or bottom-up, or both at the same time. Its political valence depends on who is seeking multicultural representation, from what social position, in response to what hegemonies, in relation to which disciplines and institutions, as part of what political project, using what means, toward what end, deploying what discourse, and so forth." Shohat goes on to claim that we cannot "discipline the anarchic dissemination of such a slippery concept as multiculturalism" because it has not adequately defined itself.

5. Ahmad (1992) critiqued Jameson's allegories that do not represent the variety of cultural practices in the third world.

6. One of the great truths of Spivak's reading of Mahasweta Devi's work is the totally banal conclusion that anticolonial nationalism was an elite configuration, the general judgment of most historians, Indian and Western alike.

7. A prime example of this process can be seen in Ashis Nandy's analysis of Rammohun Roy in *The Intimate Enemy* (1983).

8. This subtext informs a work such as Zantop's *Colonial Fantasies* (1997), where a German fictional literature on colonialism can be telescoped to show the ways in which Foucauldian fantasies of power can function even in a vacuum. The German *imaginaire* is the focus of discussion rather than any historical reality of colonialism, and the Holocaust becomes the inevitable case where such fantasies are unleashed upon reality.

9. A summary review of past scholarship.

10. This pretense is fairly common and self-serving. I remember taking part in a discussion while on the board of a national literary organization regarding the site of its next conference. One of the themes of the conference was the "subaltern." None of the board members seemed to find it odd that they were planning to hold a conference dealing with issues of alterity and subalternity in luxury hotels of the Club Med variety in a third-world site. They were primarily interested in the good hotel rates and child-friendly amenities. When I raised the absurdity of this plan with the board, the then president, a prominent American deconstructionist, remarked that it is often best to critique imperialism from within.

11. It should be noted that the term *neocolonialism* is itself an aggrandizing and inapposite term for phenomena such as globalism, the predominance of service economics, the progress of economic processes centered on information processing, and the fusion of consumer and popular cultures worldwide.

12. Timothy Brennan views it as a form of "liberal racism" that reproduces social exclusion rather than enhances diversity (Brennan 1997:115).

13. For an examination of Indian racial ideology and its scriptural justifications, see Figueira 2002.

CHAPTER 4

1. This wide-ranging fascistic impulse can also be evinced in many affirmative action hirings where the white power structure seeks the least competent minority candidate to hire in order to validate its own racist beliefs or the least competent female hire to gratify its sexism.

2. It is only recently that this demographic is being reconfigured, corrected so to speak, as nonprofessional cousins from the diaspora (notably Uganda and Kenya) migrate to join families settled in the States (Prashad 2000:78).

3. In his seminal book of the same title published in 1978, Edward Said defined "Orientalism" as the systematic stereotyping and degradation of the East that enabled Western colonial powers to victimize their subjects and consolidate hegemonic control. In the last two decades, practitioners of the critique of Orientalism have cataloged

the myriad and grave sins of the West to such a degree that one might say that they have trivialized the discussion, engendering a form of fetishism wherein all current third-world ills are traced back to colonial oppression.

4. Area studies programs were also funded by private corporations and scholarly organizations such as the Ford, Rockefeller, and Carnegie Foundations.

5. In this respect, Spivak calls to mind Foucault's rhetorical positioning of the subject in terms of power relations between the dominator and the dominated (Rapaport 2001:84).

6. The Subaltern Studies Collective, based in New Delhi, published a series of volumes in the eighties. This group was made up of social scientists such as Ranajit Guha, Partha Chatterjee, Gyanendra Pandey, and David Arnold. It began with the goal of developing a critique of colonialist and nationalist perspectives in the historiography of colonized countires.

7. It is significant to note that Bhabha's concept of hybridity is not defined in terms of genuine social analysis.

8. Following this logic, one could trace the origins of cultural studies back even to a figure such as the French collaborationist writer Robert Brasillach, whose interest in film and popular culture melded with his fascist sensibility and sexualization of authoritarian politics.

9. Cultural studies has had considerable impact on anthropology, where fieldwork, formerly a concrete place of research, could now be conceptualized as a methodological focus on hybridity and cosmopolitan experiences as much as rooted, native experiences (Clifford 1992:101). Anthropology began to speak to traveling cultures, migration, exile, diaspora, and borderlands.

10. The fate of Russian and Slavic departments in the nineties, even noteworthy programs in locales with significant numbers of heritage language students, offers ample evidence of this trend.

11. Said clearly linked his critique of Orientalism historically to area studies. This incipient link between colonial discourse and area studies has been largely ignored in subsequent postcolonial studies.

12. One has only to look at religion and anthropology curricula and recent job listings in these fields as well as conference topics.

13. I base this assertion on personal experiences I have had within comparative literature departments in several large universities.

14. One can, of course, attribute the lack of viable dissertation topics also to a general deemphasis on a sufficient number of significant texts taught in English departments and a rupture of the transmission of the tradition of close readings (with commentary) under direction and with peers.

15. During a recent medical leave, a substitute teacher, a comparatist trained in cultural studies, filled in for me. The course I had planned and initiated dealt with Greek and Sanskrit drama and theory. My substitute was responsible for assigning the final paper topic and asked students to analyze a Sanskrit play by comparing it to an American film. Given the wealth of theoretical works and dramatic literature they had read from these ancient traditions throughout the semester, I found this assignment

curious. Since courtesans appear in several ancient Sanskrit plays, I received several papers comparing Sudraka's *The Little Clay Cart* (fifth century) to Julia Roberts' star vehicle, *Pretty Woman*. This example points to a certain dumbing down or refusal/ inability to deal with the Other in its historicity and specificity or only through the optic of how it compares to some Western model.

16. Guillermo Gomez-Peña and Papon Osorio.

17. See respectively Said 1978:1–28; Bhabha 1994:6–18; and Spivak 2003: 92–97.

18. In the quoted passage, Gorra's immediate subject is Rushdie's fiction and characters.

19. On an ironic note, Jonathan Culler, the eminent comparatist who did much to popularize deconstruction in America, also weighs in on how the discipline should be restructured. Spivak ingenuously calls for a return to a traditional form of comparative literature. Culler offers a more "radical" suggestion. He wants to repackage European studies along the lines of area studies and thus reconfigure pedagogy and research in terms of discrete national entities (Harootunian 2002:104). Several points are interesting here. First, this critic clearly never fully grasped that area studies was tainted. Second, we have a situation where major proponents of critical schools feel it necessary to jettison their theories and what their theories have spawned and, once the academic "fortunes" have been made, return to their origins.

20. "Brahminization" actually refers to the entire appropriation of the Other dating back to structuralism and extending beyond postcolonial criticism. In other words, there is nothing specifically "Indian" about this process. I see it as a herme-neutical ploy of all poststructuralist criticism.

21. In *Religion and Society among the Coorgs of South India*, Srinivas defined Sanskritization as follows: "A low caste was able in a generation or two to rise to a higher position in the hierarchy by adopting vegetarianism and teetotalism, by San-skritizing its ritual and pantheon, took over as far as possible the customs, rites and beliefs of the Brahmins" (1952:30).

22. In early formulations of his theory, Srinivas favored the term *Sanskritiza-tion*. Although Srinivas admitted that 'brahminization' more accurately described the process of emulating the highest group (Srinivas 1956), the term 'Sanskritization' is more commonly used by anthropologists. As my argument deals directly with issues of textuality, I have chosen to adopt 'brahminization,' to reflect the critics' position as custodian of texts.

23. The highest of the four hierarchical classes, brahmins are especially revered. Their power was codified in their myth of origin, the *Puruṣa Sūkta* of the *Rig Veda* (10.90). Brahmins came into being from the sacrificial dismemberment of the pri-mordial man. They sprang from the head; the other castes, from the lower portions of the body. The brahmins are the custodians of the Vedas, the oldest scriptures of Hinduism revealed by God at creation. Since the Vedas traditionally did not exist in written form, the brahmins (who alone knew the texts) controlled their access and interpretation. They wielded Vedic knowledge ruthlessly, preventing nonbrahmins from studying scripture rationally. Throughout history, brahmin power has been challenged.

In the nineteenth century especially, reformers such as Rammohun Roy and Dayanand Saraswati sought to curtail brahmin hermeneutical control by establishing written texts of the Vedas and disseminating them to the faithful in vernacular translations. These Hindu reformers, along with low-caste dissidents/reformers such as Jotirao Phule and B. R. Ambedkar, felt that brahmins manipulated and distorted authoritative texts out of greed and ignorance. As preceptors, brahmins were believed to engage in hypocritical and fraudulent behavior. They were thought to have abused their privileges and, in the process, destroyed Vedic knowledge. Reformers believed that brahmins contrived to undermine and repress all dissenting voices. They prevented people from educating themselves. They wrangled over trifles and misdirected the power placed in their hands (Figueira 2002:114). They define, regulate, and speak for the nonbrahmin Other.

24. I leave to the reader to decide the extent to which literary theorists of any number of critical schools emulate the sorry behavior that Hindu reformers have ascribed to brahmins.

CHAPTER 5

1. By "migrancy," I refer to the state of being attributed to the intellectual exile, the poetic nomad, and the metaphorical traveler of recent theory.

2. Discrete identities as necessary building blocks of criticism are repudiated (Butler 1990). Manichean approaches are deemed alteritist, perpetualizing the rigidity of the Self/Other binarism governing the traditional discourse on colonialism (Suleri 1992:11; cited in Miller 1998:172). Feminists have made the astute point that just as women were discovering their subjectivity and identity, male theorists were advocating that the subject was in dire need of deconstruction and decentering (Wolff 1993:234). Susan Bordo noted that this timing was suspicious. "Gender" was all of a sudden being discussed in terms of "genders" at the moment when women were gaining some power in critical discourse and academic institutions (Bordo 1990; cited in Wolff 1993:234).

3. Said's notion of the exile is not to be confused with traveling theory that addresses the issue of when theories move out of their original context and become degraded, subdued, and tame—an academic substitute for the real thing (Said 2000:436).

4. It is very interesting that the trope of the mimic man in Naipaul is the very theme that has catapulted Homi Bhabha to fame. Their distinct representation of mimicry may account, in part, for Naipaul's negative reception in academic circles and Bhabha's iconic status within colonial discourse analysis.

5. Deleuze and Guattari differentiate the primitive or natives whose preconscious thought is made explicit by the Western interpreter from the animal-raising nomad who is warlike as opposed to the "hunter-nomad" (Miller 1998:184).

6. Scholars of Deleuze and Guattari distinguish between these theorists' intentions and the distortions of their English translator and editor.

7. As Miller points out (1998:175), in his introduction Massumi presents nomadic thought as elusive and quirky. It cannot be pinned down as in his following statement: "Representation must—even as it is being 'replaced'—be affirmed with the new equation of nomadic thought: '... +y+z+a+ ... (arm + brick + winds + ...)' " (Deleuze and Guattari: 1987:xiii).

8. Given the sufferings of the Roma and Sinti in the twentieth century, this analogy shows a certain insensitivity, reminiscent of the discourse on metaphorical exiles.

9. For a substantial critique of Miller's reading of Deleuzian nomadology, see Bogue 2007.

10. Miller claims that Deleuze and Guattari make very little effort to "strangle" the representational, anthropological, historicist, and Orientalist documentation they use. In fact, they end up reproducing this discourse in their embrace of its primitivism, dualism, and universalism (Miller 1998:205). Their nomadology might have remained relatively pure had they not availed themselves of exoticist anthropological studies on nomads or left this dimension out of their footnotes: in other words, if they had remained pure philosophers. But, they apparently wanted it both ways. Deleuze and Guattari sought to propose a pure idea of the nomad and support it with anthropological information (Miller 1998:198). The problem is that their data is tainted by the most territorializing and antinomadic project of all, colonialism.

CHAPTER 6

1. For an example of this process, see Ali Behdad's reading of the postcard representations of Algerian women (Behdad 2000:76).

2. In a number of institutions, smaller foreign language departments with decreasing enrollments were not replacing lost faculty lines. As these departments lost critical mass, they ceased being free-standing departments or programs and were absorbed into larger "foreign language" or "language and literature" departments. The crisis was particularly acute for minor languages. However, even language departments such as Slavic and German languages in demographic areas where they had been particularly strong suffered retrenchment.

3. One can add to this commentary the remarks by the now discredited University of Colorado professor Ward Churchill regarding the victims' status as "little Eichmanns." For a compendium of academic responses, see Martin and Neal 2001:13–29.

4. As an addenda to the report, Martin and Neal included positive and negative responses that the initial report elicited (Martin and Neal 2001:30–43).

5. The ACTA Report did, in fact, present more than one hundred academic responses to September 11. The original version of the report had included the names of the speakers "for purposes of documentation." These names were then deleted from subsequent versions in order to "focus discussion on the content of the views expressed" (Martin and Neal 2001:9).

6. Anouar Majid has pointed out that the legitimacy of postcolonial studies after September 11 in many respects resembles that of postmodernist discourse after the Sokal article appeared in *Social Text* (Majid 2002:11). The glaring fraudulence of both theoretical schools became crystal clear.

7. Impassioned rhetoric has always been a hallmark of Fallaci's journalism and would surely be the effect desired by any editor who would have commissioned her to write on such a topic.

8. Fallaci's commentary, the ensuing debate raging over her having exceeded the limits of acceptable speech, and the suits brought against her in France took place at the same time that France was experiencing and not responding adequately to its most sustained outbreak of racial violence since World War II. Caldwell has noted that between October 2000 and October 2002, one thousand incidents took place throughout France.

9. Stimpson made this comment at a symposium held at the University of Chicago (11 April 2003) on the fate of theory. A sound-bite synopsis of the proceedings can be found in Eakin 2003. Video files of the conference itself can be found at http://www.uchicago.edu/research/jnl-crit-inq/features/sympvideo.html (*Critical Inquiry* 2003).

CHAPTER 7

1. One can multiply these gestural episodes, as in Todd Gitlin's discussion on how similar attitudes derailed curriculum reform in California (Gitlin 1995). Gitlin writes an extensive history of Houghton Mifflin's 1990 curriculum battle in Oakland, California, over the revision of textbooks, where history needed to be reconfigured as an ethnic "feel good" experience. History is often now seen by public school administrators as an opportunity to make ethnic groups feel proud of their historical records. What is important is one's subject position. In order to attain this end, history must be presented from the victims' point of view in order to privilege their stories.

2. Under instigation of the Shiv Sena and the BJP, the name of Bombay was changed to reflect an India before the "usurpation" of the Muslims.

3. To highlight how fluid U.S. notions of race and ethnicity are, I can recount my own "minority" history. In essence, I am a poster girl for the advantages and disadvantages of affirmative action. On my mother's side, I am Italian-American. My father was born and raised in what was then British Guiana; he was a creole, descended from Portuguese forebears who had settled in Brazil and moved northward some time between the sixteenth and twentieth centuries. Growing up in the sixties in upstate New York, I definitely felt exotic among the children of Anglo-Saxon and European Jewish refugee professionals surrounding me. In this setting, we were a lower-middle-class extended family of vague ethnicity. In the late sixties, the guidance counselor in the local public high school thought that my future was to be found in the field of cosmetology. It seemed that everything about me, from the number of vowels in my

name to my economic class, suggested as much. My mother had different thoughts. Between high school and a state scholarship- and loan-funded BA from a prestigious female college, I became bureaucratically "Othered." It was the midseventies. Although my brothers, who were five and seven years my senior, had never benefited from affirmative action, suddenly I found myself an official minority. I had always been treated as one, as had the entire family, with the social slights, oddly offensive comments, and exclusionary treatment endured. But now, because it was 1976 and my father had been born in South America, I alone in the family was a certified victim of racial discrimination. Snatched from the jaws of a likely career in cosmetology, I suddenly served a cosmetic purpose. So I began my graduate and professional career as a minority female. Until the PhD, my funding consisted of merit awards and partial scholarships, although at Harvard Divinity School, a theologian of German descent trained during the Nazi era, did ask me if I was one of the new "token" students. My PhD was fully funded as a minority with a dean asking me at my first reception if I was "the Puerto Rican girl who wanted to study Sanskrit." Such an instance of class, caste, and racial ambiguity could never occur in India.

4. Very early on in the process of affirmative action, race norming became a common practice. Race norming consists of separate percentile rankings according to racial group. It allowed individuals to be ranked within their own groups, rather than in a common pool. Race norming was banned by the Civil Rights Act of 1991 as discriminatory. To bypass it, institutions sought representation by setting off searches for nonobjective criteria, as in Indian attempts to circumvent court limitations on group preferences. In essence, race norming reappeared under other names.

5. A recent study cited in the *New York Times* discusses the negative effects of shifting in law schools and the manner in which it impacts on blacks becoming lawyers (Liptak 2005).

6. I know firsthand from my days as a CIC Minority Scholarship recipient that for every three lower-class girls attending an Ivy-League institution in America today, there are ten students from middle-class backgrounds. There are sometimes "minorities" from quite privileged backgrounds, like the girl whose father was an ambassador to Italy from a South American junta regime. In the brochure introducing the recipients, she listed dressage, snorkling, and caving as her hobbies.

7. Similarly, women are expected to have research and teaching interests that engage gender issues. It has been my experience on numerous occasions to be asked in literature job interviews why I do not teach Sanskrit female poets. My interviewers are obviously unaware of the historically exclusionary status of the Sanskrit language. Balkanization also applies to ethnicity. On religion job interviews, I have been asked because of my Portuguese surname if I do liberation theology, although nothing on my resume suggests an interest in Christianity.

8. During an actual interview at a large state research university, I was informed that, due to my credentials and publications, I could not, as they had hoped, be hired as a "target of opportunity" but, rather, would have to be put in the "real" hire pool.

CONCLUSION

1. Segalen 1995:750–51: "L'exotisme n'est donc pas cet état kaléidoscopique du touriste et du médiocre spectateur, mais la réaction vive et curieuse au choc d'une individualité forte contre une objectivité dont elle perçoit et déguste la distance . . . L'exotisme n'est donc pas une adaptation; n'est donc pas la compréhension parfaite d'un hors soi-même qu'on étreindrait en soi, mais la perception aiguë et immédiate d'une incompréhensibilité éternelle. Partons donc de cet aveu d'inpénétrabilité. Ne nous flattons pas d'assimiler les moeurs, les races, les nations, les autres."

2. See Benjamin's essay "Unpacking My Library: A Talk about Book Collecting," in Benjamin 1968:67; cited in Schor 1994:254.

3. This concept of self-fashioning has also been articulated by Baudrillard who claims that collecting is always directed toward oneself, even if a collection may speak to others (Baudrillard 1994:22). The "miracle" of collecting is that it is invariably oneself that one collects (Baudrillard 1994:12). One is driven to collect in order to construct an alternative discourse that is entirely amenable insofar as it is the collector who dictates the signifiers, the ultimate signified being none other than the collector himself (Baudrillard 1994:24).

4. Stewart and Baudrillard share the belief that collecting is a degraded form of consumption. From a Marxist perspective, Stewart views the collector as a bourgeois subject.

5. See http://www.wordswithoutborders.org/.

6. Also significant is that the name alludes to the noble humanitarian struggle of *Medecins sans Frontières*.

BIBLIOGRAPHY

Achebe, Chinua. 2000. *Home and Exile*. New York: Oxford UP.

Afzal-Khan, Fawzia, and Kalpana Seshadri-Crooks, eds. 2000. *The Pre-Occupation of Postcolonial Studies*. Durham: Duke UP.

Ahmad, Aijaz. 1992. *In Theory: Classes, Nations, Literatures*. London: Verso.

———. 1995a. "The Politics of Literary Postcoloniality." *Race and Class* 36.3: 1–20.

———. 1995b. "Post-Colonialism: What's in a Name?" *Late Imperial Culture*. Eds. Román de la Campa, E. Ann Kaplan, and Michael Sprinker. London: Verso. 11–32.

Ahrens, Rüdiger, and Laurenz Volkmann, eds. 1996. *Why Literature Matters: Theories and Functions of Literature*. Heidelberg: C. Winter.

Alarcón, Norma. 1996. "Conjugating Subjects in the Age of Multiculturalism." *Mapping Multiculturalism*. Eds. Avery F. Gordon and Christopher Newfield. Minneapolis: U Minnesota P. 127–48.

Alcoff, Linda. 1991–92. "The Problem of Speaking for Others." *Cultural Critique* 20 (Winter): 5–32.

Althusser, Louis. 1965. *Lire Le capital*. 2 vols. Paris: F. Maspero.

———. 1970. *Reading "Capital."* Trans. Ben Brewster. London: New Left Books.

Ambedkar, B. R. 1979–95. *Dr. Babasaheb Ambedkar: Writings and Speeches*, 17 vols. Ed. Vasant Moon. Mumbai: Government of Maharashtra.

Amin, Samir. 1990. "The Social Movements in the Periphery: An End to National Liberation." *Transforming the Revolution: Social Movements and the World System*. Eds. Samir Amin, Giovanni Arrighi, André Gunder Frank, and Immanuel Wallerstein. New York: Monthly Review P. 96–138.

Anderson, Benedict. 1983. *Imagined Communities: Reflections on the Origin and Spread of Nationalism*. London: Verso.

Appadurai, Arjun, ed. 1986. *The Social Life of Things: Commodities in Cultural Perspective*. Cambridge: Cambridge UP.

Appiah, Kwame Anthony. 1992. *In My Father's House: Africa in the Philosophy of Culture*. New York: Oxford UP.

———. 1997. "Cosmopolitan Patriots." *Critical Inquiry* 23.3 (Spring): 617–39.

Apter, Emily. 1995. "Comparative Exile: Margins in the History of Comparative Literature." *Comparative Literature in the Age of Multiculturalism*. Ed. Charles Bernheimer. Baltimore: Johns Hopkins UP. 86–96.

Arac, Jonathan, and Harriet Ritvo, eds. 1991. *Macropolitics of Nineteenth-Century Literature: Nationalism, Exoticism, Imperialism.* Philadelphia: U Pennsylvania P.

Ashcroft, Bill, Gareth Griffiths, and Helen Tiffin, eds. 1989. *The Empire Writes Back: Theory and Practice in Post-Colonial Literature.* New York: Routledge.

Bahri, Deepika. 1995. "Once More with Feeling: What Is Postcolonialism?" *Ariel* 26.1: 51–82.

Bakhtin, Mikhail, and P. N. Medvedev. 1985. *The Formal Method in Literary Scholarship: A Critical Introduction to Sociological Poetics.* Trans. Albert J. Wehrle. Cambridge: Harvard UP.

Bal, Mieke. 1994. "Telling Objects: A Narrative Perspective on Collecting." *The Cultures of Collecting.* Eds. John Elsner and Roger Cardinal. Cambridge: Harvard UP. 97–115.

Barber, Benjamin R. 1995. *Jihad vs. McWorld: How Globalism and Tribalism Are Reshaping the World.* New York: Times Books.

Barker, Francis, Peter Hulme, Margaret Iverson, and Diana Loxley, eds. 1985. *Europe and Its Others: Proceedings of the Essex Conference on the Sociology of Literature, July 1984.* Vol. 1. Colchester: U Essex.

Barthes, Roland. 1957. *Mythologies.* Paris: Seuil.

———. 1963. *Sur Racine.* Paris: Seuil.

———. 1964. "L'activité structuraliste." *Essais critiques.* Paris: Seuil. 213–20.

———. 1970. *S/Z.* Paris: Seuil.

———. 1975. *Roland Barthes par Roland Barthes.* Paris: Seuil.

———. 1977. *Fragments d'un discours amoureux.* Paris: Seuil.

———. 1978. *Leçon: leçon inaugurale de la Chaire de sémiologie littéraire du Collège de France, prononcée le 7 janvier 1977.* Paris: Seuil.

Baudrillard, Jean. 1968. *Le système des objets.* Paris: Gallimard.

———. 1984. "The Precession of Simulacra." *Art after Modernism: Rethinking Representation.* Ed. Brian Wallis. New York: New Museum of Contemporary Art. 253–82.

———. 1986. *Amérique.* Paris: B. Grasset.

———. 1994. "The System of Collecting." *The Cultures of Collecting.* Eds. John Elsner and Roger Cardinal. Cambridge: Harvard UP. 7–24.

———. 2002. "L'Esprit du Terrorisme." Trans. Michel Valentin. *The South Atlantic Quarterly* 101.2 (Spring): 403–15.

Beauvoir, Simone de. 1954. *Les mandarins.* Paris: Gallimard.

Behdad, Ali. 2000. "Une Pratique Sauvage: Postcolonial Belatedness and Cultural Politics." *The Pre-Occupation of Postcolonial Studies.* Eds. Fawzia Afzal-Khan, and Kalpana Seshadri-Crooks. Durham: Duke UP. 71–85.

Benjamin, Walter. 1968. *Illuminations.* Ed. and intro. Hannah Arendt. Trans. Harry Zohn. New York: Harcourt, Brace & World.

Berman, Russell A. 1989. *Modern Culture and Critical Theory: Art, Politics, and the Legacy of the Frankfurt School.* Madison: U Wisconsin P.

Bernheimer, Charles, ed. 1995. *Comparative Literature in the Age of Multiculturalism.* Baltimore: Johns Hopkins UP.

Bhabha, Homi K. 1989. "The Commitment to Theory." *Questions of Third Cinema*. Eds. Jim Pines and Paul Willemen. London: British Film Institute Pub. 111–32.

———, ed. 1990. *Nation and Narration*. New York: Routledge.

———. 1992. "Postcolonial Criticism." *Redrawing the Boundaries: The Transformation of English and American Literary Studies*. Eds. Stephen Greenblatt and Giles Gunn. New York: Modern Language Association of America. 437–65.

———. 1994. *The Location of Culture*. New York: Routledge.

———. 2003. "Making Difference: The Legacy of the Culture Wars." *Art Forum* 41.8 (Apr.): 73–76, 234–37.

Boer, Inge E. 1996. "The World beyond Our Window: Nomads, Traveling Theories and the Function of Boundaries." *Parallax: A Journal of Metadiscursive Theory and Cultural Practices* 3 (Sep.): 7–26.

Bogue, Ronald. 2007. *Deleuze's Way: Essays in Transverse Ethics and Aesthetics*. Aldershot: Ashgate.

Bongie, Chris. 1991. *Exotic Memories: Literature, Colonialism, and the Fin de Siècle*. Stanford: Stanford UP.

———. 1998. *Islands and Exiles: The Creole Identities of Post/Colonial Literature*. Stanford: Stanford UP.

Bordo, Susan. 1990. "Feminism, Postmodernism, and Gender-Scepticism." *Feminism/Postmodernism*. Ed. Linda J. Nicholson. New York: Routledge. 133–56.

Bourdieu, Pierre. 1982. *Ce que parler veut dire: L'économie des échanges linguistiques*. Paris: Fayard.

———. 1984. *Homo academicus*. Paris: Minuit.

———. 1987. *Choses dites*. Paris: Minuit

———. 1988. *Homo academicus*. Trans. Peter Collier. Stanford: Stanford UP.

———. 1991. *Language and Symbolic Power*. Ed. John B. Thompson. Trans. Gino Raymond and Matthew Adamson. Cambridge: Harvard UP.

———. 1993. *The Field of Cultural Production: Essays on Art and Literature*. Ed. Randal Johnson. New York: Columbia UP.

Bowen, William G., and Derek Bok. 1998. *The Shape of the River: Long-term Consequences of Considering Race in College and University Admissions*. Princeton: Princeton UP.

Braidotti, Rosi. 1994. *Nomadic Subjects: Embodiment and Sexual Difference in Contemporary Feminist Theory*. New York: Columbia UP.

Braudel, Fernand. 1966. *Méditerranée et le monde méditerranéen à l'époque de Philippe II*. 2nd rev. ed. Paris: A. Colin.

———. 1967. *Civilisation matérielle et capitalisme IVe-XVIIIe siècle*. Paris: A. Colin.

———. 1986. *L'identité de la France: Espace et histoire*. Paris: Flammarion.

Braverman, Amy M. 2004. "The Interpretation of Gods." *University of Chicago Magazine* 97.2 (Dec.): 32–36.

Brennan, Timothy. 1997. *At Home in the World: Cosmopolitanism Now*. Cambridge: Harvard UP.

Brewer, Dominic J., Eric R. Eide, and Dan D. Goldhaber. *An Examination of the Role of Student Race and Ethnicity in Higher Education Since 1972*. 1999. Washington, DC: The Rand Corporation.

Brown, Michael K., Martin Carnoy, Elliot Currie, Troy Dusher, David B. Oppenheimer, Marjorie M. Schultz, David Wellman. 2003. *Whitewashing Race: The Myth of a Color-Blind Society.* Berkeley: U California P.

Butler, Judith. 1990. *Gender Troubles: Feminism and the Subversion of Identity.* New York: Routledge.

Caillois, Roger. 1 Dec. 1954 and 1 Jan. 1955. "Illusions à rebours." *Nouvelle Revue Française* 24–25: 1010–24, 58–70.

———. 1974. "La réponse de R. Caillois." *Le Monde,* 28 Jun.

Caldwell, Christopher. 2002a. "Allah Mode: France's Islam Problem." *The Weekly Standard* 7.42 (15 Jul.): 20–26.

———. 2002b. "The Fallaci Affair." *Commentary* 114.3 (Oct.): 34–44.

Callinicos, Alex. 1976. *Althusser's Marxism.* London: Pluto P.

———. 1989. *Against Postmodernism: A Marxist Critique.* Cambridge: Polity P.

———. 1995. "Wonders Taken for Signs: Homi Bhabha's Postcolonialism." *Post-ality: Marxism and Postmodernism.* Eds. Mas'ud Zavarzadeh, Teresa L. Ebert, and Donald Morton. Washington, D.C.: Maisonneuve P. 98–112.

Campa, Román de la, E. Ann Kaplan, and Michael Sprinker, eds. 1995. *Late Imperial Culture.* London: Verso.

Canguilhem, Georges. 1966. *Le normal et le pathologique.* Paris: Presses Universitaires de France.

Carroll, Lucy. 1977. " 'Sanskritization,' 'Westernization' and 'Social Mobility': A Reappraisal of the Relevance of Anthropological Concepts to the Social Historian of Modern India." *Journal of Anthropological Research* 33.4 (Winter): 355–71.

Centre for Contemporary Cultural Studies. 1982. *The Empire Strikes Back: Race and Racism in 70s Britain.* London: Hutchinson.

Césaire, Aimé. 1950. *Discours sur le colonialisme.* Paris: Réclame.

Chakrabarty, Dipesh. 1992a. "Postcoloniality and the Artifice of History: Who Speaks for 'Indian' Pasts?" *Representations* 37 (Winter): 1–26.

———. 1992b. "The Death of History? Historical Consciousness and the Culture of Late Capitalism." *Public Culture* 4.2 (Spring): 47–65.

Chambers, Iain, and Lidia Curti, eds. 1996. *The Post-Colonial Question: Common Skies, Divided Horizons.* London: Routledge.

Chatterjee, Partha. 1986. *Nationalist Thought and the Colonial World: A Derivative Discourse.* London: Zed Books.

———. 1993. *The Nation and Its Fragments: Colonial and Postcolonial Histories.* Princeton: Princeton UP.

Chomsky, Noam. 1982. *Towards a New Cold War: Essays on the Current Crisis and How We Got There.* New York: Pantheon Books.

———. 2001. *9-11.* New York: Seven Stories P.

Chow, Rey. 1993. *Writing Diaspora: Tactics of Intervention in Contemporary Cultural Studies.* Bloomington: Indiana UP.

———. 1995. "The Fascist Longings in Our Midst." *Ariel* 26.1 (Jan.): 23–50.

———. 2002. "Theory, Area Studies, Cultural Studies: Issues of Pedagogy in Multiculturalism." *Learning Places: The Afterlives of Area Studies.* Eds. Masao Miyoshi and H. D. Harootunian. Durham: Duke UP. 103–18.

Chrisman, Laura. 1993. "Theorizing 'Race,' Racism and Culture: Pitfalls of Idealist Critiques." *Paragraph: A Journal of Modern Critical Theory* 16.1: 78–90.

———. 1997a. "Gendering Imperial Culture: King Solomon's Mines and Feminist Criticisms." *Cultural Readings of Imperialism: Edward Said and the Gravity of History.* Eds. Keith Ansell-Pearson, Benita Parry, and Judith Squires. London: Lawrence & Wishart. 290–304.

———. 1997b. "Journeying to Death: Gilroy's *Black Atlantic.*" *Race and Class* 39.2: 51–64.

The Civil War Courier. 2000. 16 (Dec.).

———. 2002. 18.7 (Aug.).

Clark, John. 1996. "On Two Books by Edward W. Said." *Bicitra Seni* 2 [Universiti Sains Malaysia] (Jun.): 20–47.

Clifford, James. 1988. *The Predicament of Culture: Twentieth-Century Ethnography, Literature, and Art.* Cambridge: Harvard UP.

———. 1992. "Traveling Theories." *Cultural Studies.* Eds. Lawrence Grossberg, Cary Nelson, and Paula A. Treichler. London: Routledge. 96–111.

———, and George Marcus, eds. 1986. *Writing Culture: The Poetics and Politics of Ethnography.* Berkeley: U California P.

Constable, Nicole. 1997. *Maid to Order in Hong Kong: Stories of Filipina Workers.* Ithaca: Cornell UP.

Cornell, Drucilla, Michel Rosenfeld, and David Gray Carlson, eds. 1992. *Deconstruction and the Possibility of Justice.* New York: Routledge.

Coward, Rosalind, and John Ellis. 1977. *Language and Materialism: Developments in Semiology and the Theory of the Subject.* London: Routledge & Paul.

Critical Inquiry. 2003. "Editorial Board Symposium, 11 April 2003." (Quick-Time MOV files). *Critical Inquiry* 30.2: http://www.uchicago.edu/research/ jnl-crit-inq/features/sympvideo.html.

Cruz, Jon. 1996. "From Farce to Tragedy: Reflections on the Reification of Race at Century's End." *Mapping Multiculturalism.* Eds. Avery F. Gordon and Christopher Newfield. Minneapolis: U Minnesota P. 19–39.

Davis, Angela Y. 1996. "Gender, Class, Multiculturalism" Rethinking 'Race' Politics." *Mapping Multiculturalism.* Eds. Avery F. Gordon and Christopher Newfield. Minneapolis: U Minnesota P. 40–48.

Deleuze, Gilles. 1973. "Pensée nomade." *Nietzsche aujourd'hui? Exposés.* Ed. Pierre Boudot. 2 vols. Paris: Union générale d'éditions. 1: 159–74.

———, and Félix Guattari. 1980. *Milles plateaux: Capitalisme et schizophrénie.* Paris: Minuit.

———. 1987. *A Thousand Plateaus: Capitalism and Schizophrenia.* Trans. Brian Massumi. Minneapolis: U Minnesota P.

de Man, Paul. 1971. *Blindness and Insight: Essays in the Rhetoric of Contemporary Criticism.* New York: Oxford UP.

Denzin, Norman K., and Yvonna S. Lincoln, eds. 2003. *9/11 in American Culture.* Walnut Creek: AltaMira P.

Derrida, Jacques. 1967. *De la grammatologie.* Paris: Minuit.

———. 1972a [1968]. "La pharmacie de Platon." *La Dissémination.* Paris: Seuil. 71–197.

———. 1972b. *Marges de la philosophie*. Paris: Minuit.

———. 1972c. *Positions: Entretiens avec Henri Ronse, Julia Kristeva, Jean-Louis Houdebine, Guy Scarpetta*. Paris: Minuit.

———. 1978. *Éperons: Les styles de Nietzsche*. Paris: Flammarion.

———. 1989. "Three Questions to Hans-Georg Gadamer." *Dialogue and Deconstruction: The Gadamer-Derrida Encounter*. Eds. Diane P. Michelfelder and Richard E. Palmer. Albany: State U New York P. 52–54.

———. 1992. "Force of Law: The Mystical Foundation of Authority." *Deconstruction and the Possibility of Justice*. Eds. Drucilla Cornell, Michel Rosenfeld, and David Gray Carlson. New York: Routledge. 3–67.

———. 1993. *Spectres de Marx: L'état de la dette, le travail du deuil et la nouvelle Internationale*. Paris: Galilée.

———. 1994. *Politiques de l'amitié: Suivi de L'oreille de Heidegger*. Paris: Galilée.

———. 1999. "Marx and Sons." *Ghostly Demarcations: A Symposium on Jacques Derrida's Spectres of Marx*. Ed. Michael Sprinker. New York: Verso. 213–69.

Dews, Peter. 1987. *Logics of Disintegration: Post-Structuralist Thought and the Claims of Critical Theory*. London: Verso.

Dirlik, Arif. 1987. "Culturalism as Hegemonic Ideology and Liberating Practice." *Cultural Critique* 6 (Spring): 13–50.

———. 1994. "The Postcolonial Aura: Third World Criticism in the Age of Global Capitalism." *Critical Inquiry* 20.2 (Winter): 328–56.

———. 1997. *The Postcolonial Aura: Third World Criticism in the Age of Global Capitalism*. Boulder: Westview P.

———. 2001. "Colonialism, Globalization and Culture: Reflections on September 11th." *Recherche littéraire/Literary Research* 18.36: 244–54.

Donaghue, Denis. 1987. "A Criticism of One's Own." *Men in Feminism*. Eds. Alice Jardine and Paul Smith. New York: Methuen. 146–52.

Dosse, François. 1991–92. *Histoire du structuralisme*. 2 vols. Paris: Editions la Découverte.

———. 1997. *History of Structuralism*. 2 vols. Trans. Deborah Glassman. Minneapolis: U Minnesota P.

D'Souza, Dinesh. 1991. *Illiberal Education: The Politics of Race and Sex on Campus*. New York: Free P.

Du Bois, W. E. B. 1985. *Against Racism: Unpublished Essays, Papers, Addresses, 1887–1961*. Ed. Herbert Aptheker. Amherst: U Massachusetts P.

du Cille, Ann. 1997. "The Occult of True Womanhood." *Female Subjects in Black and White: Race, Psychoanalysis, Feminism*. Eds. Elizabeth Abel, Barbara Christian, and Helena Moglen. Berkeley: U California P. 21–56.

Duvignaud. Jean. 1975. "Esquisse pour le nomade." *Nomades et vagabonds*. Eds. Jacques Berque, et al. Paris: Union générale d'éditions. 13–40.

Eagleton, Terry. 1990. *Nationalism, Colonialism, and Literature*. Intro. Seamus Deane. Minneapolis: U Minnesota P.

———. 1991. *Ideology: An Introduction*. London: Verso.

Eakin, Emily. 2003. "The Latest Theory Is That Theory Doesn't Matter." *New York Times*, 19 Apr.

Elsner, John, and Roger Cardinal, eds. 1994. *The Cultures of Collecting.* Cambridge: Harvard UP.

Erlanger, Steven. 2001. "A Nation Challenged: Voices of Opposition; In Europe, Some Critics Say the Attacks Stemmed from American Failings." *New York Times,* 22 Sep.

Essed, Philomena. 1991. *Understanding Everyday Racism: An Interdisciplinary Theory.* Newbury Park: Sage.

Fallaci, Oriana. 2001. *La Rabbia e l'orgoglio.* Milan: Rizzoli.

———. 2002. *The Rage and the Pride.* New York: Rizzoli.

Fanon, Franz. 1961. *Les Damnés de la terre.* Paris: F. Maspero.

———. 1963. *The Wretched of the Earth.* Trans. Constance Farrington. New York: Grove P.

Fields, Barbara Jean. 1990. "Slavery, Race and Ideology in the United States." *New Left Review* 181 (May–Jun.): 95–118.

Figueira, Dorothy. 1994. *The Exotic: A Decadent Quest.* Albany: State U New York P.

———. 2000. "The Profits of Postcolonialism." *Comparative Literature* 52.3: 246–54.

———. 2002. *Aryans, Jews, Brahmins: Theorizing Authority through Myths of Identity.* Albany: State U New York P.

Fish, Stanley. 1997. "Boutique Multiculturalism or Why Liberals Are Incapable of Thinking about Hate Speech." *Critical Inquiry* 23 (Winter): 378–95.

Fluck, Winfried. 1990. "The Americanization of Literary Studies." *American Studies International* 28.2: 9–22.

———. 1992. "The 'Americanization' of History in New Historicism." *Monatshefte für Deutschen Unterricht, Deutsche Sprache und Literatur* 84.2: 220–28.

———. 1996. "Literature, Liberalism, and the Current Cultural Radicalism." *Why Literature Matters: Theories and Functions of Literature.* Eds. Rüdiger Ahrens and Laurenz Volkmann. Heidelberg: C. Winter. 211–34.

Ford, Boris, ed. 1988. *American Literature.* Vol. 9 of *The New Pelican Guide to English Literature.* London: Penguin.

Foucault, Michel. 1969. *L'Archéologie du savoir.* Paris: Gallimard.

———. 1972. *The Archaeology of Knowledge.* Trans. A. M. Sheridan Smith. New York: Pantheon Books.

———. 1975. *Surveiller et punir: Naissance de la prison.* Paris: Gallimard.

———. 1979. *Discipline and Punish: The Birth of the Prison.* Trans. A. M. Sheridan Smith. New York: Vintage Books.

———. 1976. *Histoire de la sexualité.* Paris: Gallimard.

———. 1990–92. *The History of Sexuality.* 3 vols. Trans. Robert Hurley. London: Penguin.

Fox-Genovese, Elizabeth. 1986. "The Claims of a Common Culture: Gender, Race, Class, and the Canon." *Salmagundi* 72 (Fall): 131–43.

Frankenberg, Ruth, and Lata Mani. 1993. "Crosscurrents, Crosstalk: Race, 'Postcoloniality' and the Politics of Location." *Cultural Studies* 7.2: 292–310.

Freund, Charles Paul. 2001. "2001 Nights: The End of the Orientalist Critique." *Reason* (Dec.): http://reason.com/0112/cr.cf.2001.shtml.

Fukuyama, Francis. 2001. "Le choc de l'Islam et de la modernité." *Le Figaro,* Nov. 26. http://www.lefigaro.fr/.

Furet, François. 1979. *Penser la revolution française.* Paris: Gallimard.

———. 1982. *L'atelier de l'histoire.* Paris: Flammarion.

Gabel, Joseph. 1975. *False Consciousness: An Essay on Reification.* Trans. Margaret A. Thompson. Oxford: Blackwell.

Galanter, Marc. 1984. *Competing Equalities: Law and the Backward Classes in India.* Berkeley: U California P.

Gates, Henry Louis. 1988. *The Signifying Monkey: A Theory of Afro-American Literary Criticism.* New York: Oxford UP.

———. 1992. "Pluralism and Its Discontents." *Contention: Debates in Society, Culture, and Science* 2.1 (Fall): 69–79.

Gauguin, Paul. 1984. *Correspondence de Paul Gauguin: Document, témoignages.* Ed. Victor Merlhès. Paris: Fondation Singer-Polignac.

Georgia League of the South. n.d. Pamphlet. GA League of the South. PO Box 1263 McDonough, GA 30253.

Ghosh, Partha S. 1996. "Language Policy and National Integration." *Ethnic Studies Report* 24.1: 49–72.

Giraud-Boura, André. 1972. *Origines de l'occident: Nomades et sédentaires.* Paris: Weber.

Giroux, Henry A. 1992. "Post-Colonial Ruptures and Democratic Possibilities: Multi-culturalism as Anti-Racist Pedagogy." *Cultural Critique* (Spring): 5–39.

———. 1995. "National Identity and the Politics of Multiculturalism." *College Literature* 22.2 (Jun.): 42–57.

Gitlin, Todd. 1995. *The Twilight of Common Dreams: Why America Is Wracked by Culture Wars.* New York: Metropolitan Books.

Gordon, Avery F., and Christopher Newfield, eds. 1996. *Mapping Multiculturalism.* Minneapolis: U Minnesota P.

Gorra, Michael. 1997. *After Empire: Scott, Naipaul, Rushdie.* Chicago: U Chicago P.

Greenblatt, Stephen. 1990. *Learning to Curse: Essays in Early Modern Culture.* New York: Routledge.

Grewal, Inderpal. 1994. "The Postcolonial, Ethnic Studies, and the Diaspora: The Contexts of Ethnic Immigration/Migrant Cultural Studies in the US." *Socialist Review* 24.4: 45–74.

Grossberg, Lawrence, Cary Nelson, and Paula A. Treichler, eds. 1992. *Cultural Studies.* New York: Routledge.

Guerrero, M. Annette Jaimes. 1996. "American Indian Studies and Multiculturalism." *Mapping Multiculturalism.* Eds. Avery F. Gordon and Christopher Newfield. Minneapolis: U Minnesota P. 49–63.

Guha, Ranajit. 1997. "Not at Home in Empire." *Critical Inquiry* 23.3: 482–93.

———, ed. 1982–90. *Subaltern Studies.* 4 vols. Delhi: Oxford UP.

Guillory, John. 1993. *Cultural Capital: The Problem of Literary Canon Formation.* Chicago: U Chicago P.

Gutmann, Amy. 1994. "Introduction." *Multiculturalism: Examining the Politics of Recognition.* Charles Taylor. Ed. Amy Gutmann. Princeton: Princeton UP. 3–24.

Habermas, Jürgen. 1998. "Struggles for Recognition in the Democratic Constitutional State." *Multiculturalism: Examining the Politics of Recognition.* Charles Taylor. Ed. Amy Gutmann. Princeton: Princeton UP. 107–48.

Hall, Stuart. 1996. " 'When was the Post-Colonial?' Thinking the Limit." *The Post-Colonial Question: Common Skies, Divided Horizons.* Eds. Iain Chambers and Lidia Curti. London: Routledge. 242–60.

Hancock, M. 1998. "Unmaking the 'Great Traditions': Ethnography, National Culture and Area Studies." *Identities: Global Studies in Power and Culture* 4.3–4 (Jun.): 343–88.

Harlow, Barbara. 1987. *Resistance Literature.* New York: Methuen.

Harootunian, H. D. 2002. "Postcoloniality's Unconscious/Area Studies' Desire." *Learning Places: The Afterlives of Area Studies.* Eds. Masao Miyoshi and H. D. Harootunian. Durham: Duke UP. 150–74.

Hartocollis, Anemona. 2001. "Campus Culture Wars Flare Anew over Tenor of Debate after the Attacks." *New York Times,* 30 Sep.

"Has Multiculturalism Failed?" 2001. *New York Times,* 18 Nov. Poll.

Heidegger, Martin. n.d. *Questions.* Vol. 1. Paris: Gallimard.

Huggan, Graham. 2000. "Exoticism, Ethnicity, and the Multicultural Fallacy." *"New" Exoticism: Changing Patterns in the Construction of Otherness.* Ed. Isabel Santaolalla. Amsterdam: Rodopi. 91–96.

———. 2001. *The Postcolonial Exotic: Marketing the Margins.* London: Routledge.

Huntington, Samuel P. 1996. *The Clash of Civilizations and the Remaking of World Order.* New York: Simon & Schuster.

Hutcheon, Linda. 1995. "Colonialism and the Postcolonial Condition." *PMLA* 110.1 (Jan.): 7–16.

———, and Marion Richmond, eds. 1990. *Other Solitudes: Canadian Multicultural Fictions.* Toronto: Oxford UP.

India. Commission for Scheduled Castes and Scheduled Tribes. 1980. *Report of the Commission for Scheduled Castes and Schedules Tribes.* First Report. Jul. 1978–Mar. 1979. New Delhi: Controller of Publication.

Isaacs, Harold. 1972. *Images of Asia: American Views of China and India.* New York: Harper & Row.

Jacoby, Russell. 1994a. *Dogmatic Wisdom: How the Culture Wars Divert Education and Distract America.* New York: Doubleday.

———. 1994b. "The Myth of Multiculturalism." *New Left Review* 208 (Nov.–Dec.): 121–26.

———. 1995. "Marginal Returns: The Trouble with Post-Colonial Theory." *Lingua Franca* 5.6: 30–37.

Jameson, Fredric. 1986. "Third World Literature in the Era of Multinational Capitalism." *Social Text* 15: 65–88.

Jhabvala, Ruth Prawer. 1986. *Out of India: Selected Stories.* New York: Morrow.

Johnson, Barbara. 1987. *A World of Difference.* Baltimore: Johns Hopkins UP.

Johnson, Beverly L. 1980. "Marital and Family Characteristics of the Labor Force, March 1979." *Monthly Labor Review* 103.4 (Apr.): 48–52.

Jordan, June. 1992. *Technical Difficulties: African American Notes on the State of the Union.* New York: Pantheon Books.

Joris, Pierre. 2003. *A Nomad Poetics: Essays.* Middletown: Wesleyan UP.

Joshi, Barbara R. 1982. "Whose Law, Whose Order: 'Untouchables,' Social Violence, and the State of India." *Asian Survey* 22.7 (Jul.): 676–87.

Judt, Tony. 1998. *The Burden of Responsibility: Blum, Camus, Aron, and the French Twentieth Century.* Chicago: U Chicago P.

Kamuf, Peggy. 1997. "Deconstruction and Feminism: A Repetition." *Feminist Interpretations of Jacques Derrida.* Ed. Nancy J. Holland. University Park: Pennsylvania State UP. 103–26.

Kaplan, Caren. 1987. "Deterritorializations: The Rewriting of Home and Exile in Western Feminist Discourse." *Cultural Critique* 6 (Spring): 187–98.

Kaplan, Robert D. 1996. *The Ends of the Earth: A Journey at the Dawn of the 21st Century.* New York: Random House.

Kotkin, Joel. 1993. *Tribes: How Race, Religion, and Identity Determine Success in the New Global Economy.* New York: Random House.

Krishnaswamy, Revathi. 1995. "Mythologies of Migrancy: Postcolonialism, Postmodernism and the Politics of (Dis)location." *Ariel* 26.1 (Jan.): 125–46.

Kristeva, Julia. 1990. *Les samouraïs: Roman.* Paris: Fayard.

Kuhn, Thomas S. 1962. *The Structure of Scientific Revolutions.* Chicago: U Chicago P.

Lacan, Jacques. 1966. *Écrits.* Paris: Seuil.

Laclau, Ernesto, and Chantal Mouffe. 1985. *Hegemony and Socialist Strategy: Towards a Radical Democratic Politics.* London: Verso.

Larsen, Neil. 2000. "DetermiNation: Postcolonialism, Poststructuralism, and the Problem of Ideology." *The Pre-Occupation of Postcolonial Studies.* Eds. Fawzia Afzal-Khan and Kalpana Seshadri-Crooks. Durham: Duke UP. 140–56.

Lazarus, Neil. 1999. *Nationalism and Cultural Practice in the Postcolonial World.* Cambridge: Cambridge UP.

Le Roy Ladurie, Emmanuel. 1975. *Montaillou, village occitan de 1294 à 1324.* Paris: Gallimard.

———. 1978. *Montaillou: Cathars and Catholics in a French Village, 1294–1324.* Trans. Barbara Bray. London: Scolar.

Lévi-Strauss, Claude. 1949. *Les structures élémentaires de la parenté.* Paris: Presses Universitaires de France.

———. 1955. *Tristes tropiques.* Paris: Plon.

———. 1969. *The Elementary Structures of Kinship.* Trans. James Harle Bell, John Richard von Sturmer, and Rodney Needham. London: Eyre & Spottiswoode.

———. 1974. *Tristes tropiques.* Trans. John and Doreen Weightman. New York: Atheneum.

Lewis, Michael J. 2002. "Mourning without Meaning." *Commentary* 114.4: 56–60.

Lilla, Mark. 2001. *The Reckless Mind: Intellectuals in Politics.* New York: New York Review of Books.

Lincoln, Bruce. 2003. *Holy Terrors: Thinking about Religion after September 11.* Chicago: U Chicago P.

Lingua Franca, ed. 2000. *The Sokal Hoax: The Sham That Shook the Academy.* Lincoln: U Nebraska P.

Lionnet, Françoise. 1989. *Autobiographical Voices: Race, Gender, Self-Portraiture.* Ithaca: Cornell UP.

Liptak, Adam. 2005. "For Blacks in Law School, Can Less be More?" *New York Times,* 13 Feb.

Loomba, Ania. 1998. *Colonialism/Postcolonialism.* London: Routledge.

Lubiano, Wahneema. 1996. "Like Being Mugged by a Metaphor: Multiculturalism and State Narratives." *Mapping Multiculturalism.* Eds. Avery F. Gordon and Christopher Newfield. Minneapolis: U Minnesota P. 64–75.

Lyotard, Jean-François. 1979. *La condition postmoderne: Rapport sur le savoir.* Paris: Minuit.

Majid, Anouar. 2002. "The Failure of Postcolonial Theory After 9/11." *Chronicle of Higher Education* 49.10 (1 Nov.): B 11–12.

Makarius, Raoul, and Laura Makarius. 1973. *Structuralisme ou ethnologie: Pour une critique radicale de l'anthropologie de Lévi-Strauss.* Paris: Anthropos.

Marable, Manning. 1992. "Debate on Multiculturalism." *Bowling Green State University News* (3 Mar.): 2.

Martin, Jerry, and Anne D. Neal. 2001. *Defending Civilization: How Our Universities Are Failing America and What Can Be Done about It.* Report. Washington DC: American Council of Trustees and Alumni.

Mathews, Nancy Mowll. 2001. *Paul Gauguin: An Erotic Life.* New Haven: Yale UP.

Mauss, Marcel. 1925. *Essai sur le don: Forme et Raison de l'échange dans les sociétés archaïques.* Paris: Alcan.

——. 1954. *The Gift: Forms and Functions of Exchange in Archaic Societies.* Trans. Ian Cunnison. Glencoe: Free P.

Mazumdar, Sucheta. 1989. "Race and Racism: South Asians in the United States." *Frontiers of Asian American Studies: Writing, Research, and Commentary.* Eds. Gail M. Nomura, Russell Endo, Stephen H. Sumida, and Russell C. Leong. Pullman: Washington State UP. 25–38.

McClintock, Anne. 1992. "The Angel of Progress: Pitfalls of the Term 'Post-Colonialism.'" *Social Text* 31–32: 84–98.

Memmi, Albert. 1965. *Colonizer and the Colonized.* Trans. Howard Greenfeld. New York: Orion P.

Menand, Louis. 1991. "The Politics of Deconstruction." Review of *Sign of the Times: Deconstruction and the Fall of Paul de Man,* by David Lehman. *New York Review of Books* 38.19 (21 Nov.): 39–45.

——. 2002. "Faith, Hope and Clarity." *New Yorker* 16 Sep.: 98–104.

Michel, Martina. 1995. "Positioning the Subject: Locating Postcolonial Studies." *Ariel* 26.1 (Jan.): 83–99.

Michelfelder, Diane P., and Richard E. Palmer, eds. 1989. *Dialogue and Deconstruction: The Gadamer-Derrida Encounter.* Albany: State U New York P.

Miller, Christopher L. 1998. *Nationalists and Nomads: Essay on Francophone African Literature and Culture.* Chicago: U Chicago P.

Mishra, Vijay, and Bob Hodge. 1991. "What Is Post(-)colonialism?" *Textual Practice* 5.3: 399–414.

Miyoshi, Masao, and H. D. Harootunian, eds. 2002. *Learning Places: The Afterlives of Area Studies.* Durham: Duke UP.

Morely, David, and Kuan-Hsing Chen, eds. 1996. *Stuart Hall: Critical Dialogues in Cultural Studies.* London: Routledge.

Morris, Meaghan. 1988. "At Henry Parkes Motel." *Cultural Studies* 2.1: 1–47.

Mouffe, Chantal. 1988. "Hegemony and New Political Subjects." *Marxism and the Interpretation of Culture.* Eds. Cary Nelson and Lawrence Grossberg. Urbana: U Illinois P. 89–101.

Mukherjee, Arun P. 1986. "Ideology in the Classroom: A Case Study in the Teaching of English Literature in Canadian Universities." *Dalhousie Review* 66.1–2: 22–30.

Mukherjee, Bharati. 1981. "An Invisible Woman." *Saturday Night* (Mar.): 36–40.

———. 1989. "Prophet and Loss: Rushdie's Migration of Souls." *Village Voice Literary Supplement* 72 (Mar.): 9–12.

Mulhern, Francis. 1992. *Contemporary Marxist Literary Criticism.* London: Longman.

———. 1995. "The Politics of Cultural Studies." *Monthly Review* 47.3 (Jul.–Aug.): 31–40.

Nancy, Jean-Luc. 1986. *La communauté désœuvrée.* Paris: C. Bourgois.

Nandy, Ashis. 1983. *The Intimate Enemy: Loss and Recovery of Self under Colonialism.* Delhi: Oxford UP.

Nash, Gary B. 1992. "The Great Multicultural Debate." *Contention* 1.3: 1–28.

Nelson, Cary, and Lawrence Grossberg, eds. 1988. *Marxism and the Interpretation of Culture.* Urbana: U Illinois P.

Nelson, Emmanuel S., ed. 1992. *Reworlding: The Literature of the Indian Diaspora.* New York: Greenwood P.

Newfield, Christopher, and Avery F. Gordon. 1996. "Multiculturalism's Unfinished Business." *Mapping Multiculturalism.* Eds. Avery F. Gordon and Christopher Newfield. Minneapolis: U Minnesota P. 76–115.

New York Times. June 19, 2008. "Group in India Ends Protests." PA 12.

Nicholson, Linda J., ed. 1990. *Feminism/Postmodernism.* New York: Routledge.

Nomura, Gail M., Russell Endo, Stephen H. Sumida, and Russell C. Leong. 1989. *Frontiers of Asian American Studies: Writing, Research, and Commentary.* Pullman: Washington State UP.

O'Brien, Mark, and Craig Little, eds. 1990. *Reimaging America: The Arts of Social Change.* Philadelphia: New Society Publishers.

Okada, Richard H. 2002. "Areas, Disciplines, and Ethnicity." *Learning Places: The Afterlives of Area Studies.* Eds. Masao Miyoshi and H. D. Harootunian. Durham: Duke UP. 190–205.

Palumbo-Liu, David. 2002. "Multiculturalism Now: Civilization, National Identity, and Difference before and after September 11th." *Boundary* 2.29.2: 109–27.

Parry, Benita. 1987. "Problems in Current Theories of Colonial Discourse." *The Oxford Literary Review* 9.1–2: 27–58.

Picard, Raymond. 1965. *Nouvelle critique ou nouvelle imposture.* Paris: J.-J. Pauvert.

Podhoretz, Norman. 2002. "The Return of the 'Jackal Bins.'" *Commentary* (Apr.): 29–39.

Prakash, Gyan, ed. 1995. *After Colonialism: Imperial Histories and Postcolonial Displacements*. Princeton: Princeton UP.

Prashad, Vijay. 2000. *The Karma of Brown Folk*. Minneapolis: U Minnesota P.

Pratt, Mary Louise. 1994. "Humanities for the Future: Reflection on the Western Culture Debate at Stanford." *Falling into Theory: Conflicting Views on Reading Literature*. Ed. David Richter. Boston: St. Martin's P. 55–63.

Probyn, Elspeth. 1990. "Travels in the Postmodern: Making Sense of the Local." *Feminism/Postmodernism*. Ed. Linda J. Nicholson. New York: Routledge. 176–89.

Propp, Vladimir. 1958. *Morphology of the Folktale*. Ed. Svatava Pirkova-Jakobson. Trans. Laurence Scott. Bloomington: Research Center, Indiana U.

———. 1983. *Les racines historiques du conte merveilleux*. Trans. Lise Gruel-Apert (from Russian). Paris: Gallimard.

———. 1984. *Theory and History of Folklore*. Trans. Ariadna Y. Martin and Robert P. Martin. Ed. Anatoly Liberman. Minneapolis: U Minnesota P.

Rabinow, Paul. 1986. "Representations Are Social Facts: Modernity and Post-Modernity in Anthropology." *Writing Culture: The Poetics and Politics of Ethnography*. Eds. James Clifford and George Marcus. Berkeley: U California P. 234–61.

Radhakrishnan, R. 1993. "Postcoloniality and Boundaries of Identity." *Callaloo* 16.4 (Fall): 750–71.

Rafael, Vicente. L. 1994. "The Cultures of Area Studies in the United States." *Social Text* 41 (Winter): 91–111.

———, ed. 1995. *Discrepant Histories: Translocal Essays on Filipino Cultures*. Philadelphia: Temple UP.

Rajan, Tilottama. 2002. *Deconstruction and the Remainders of Phenomenology: Sartre, Derrida, Foucault, Baudrillard*. Stanford: Stanford UP.

Rapaport, Herman. 2001. *The Theory Mess: Deconstruction in Eclipse*. New York: Columbia UP.

Ravitch, Diane. 1990. "Multiculturalism: E Pluribus Plures." *American Scholar* 59.3 (Summer): 337–54.

Remak, Henry H. H. 1960. "Comparative Literature at the Crossroads: Diagnosis, Theory and Prognosis." *Yearbook of Comparative and General Literature*. Vol. 9. Bloomington: Indiana U. 1–29.

———. 1978. "Exoticism in Romanticism." *Comparative Literature Studies* 15.1: 53–65.

Revel, Jean-François. 2003. *Anti-Americanism*. Trans. Diarmid Cammell. San Francisco: Encounter Books.

Rheims, Maurice. 1959. *La vie étrange des objets: Histoire de la curiosité*. Paris: Plon.

Richter, David, ed. 1994. *Falling into Theory: Conflicting Views on Reading Literature*. Boston: St. Martin's P.

Ricoeur, Paul. 1963. "Structure et herméneutique." *Esprit* 31.322 (Nov.): 596–627.

———. 1981. *Hermeneutics and the Human Sciences: Essays on Language, Action and Interpretation*. Ed. and Trans. John B. Thompson. Cambridge: Cambridge UP.

———. 1990. *Soi-même comme un autre*. Paris: Seuil.

Rizvi, Fazal. 1994. "The Arts, Education and the Politics of Multiculturalism." *Culture, Difference and the Arts.* Eds. Sneja Gunew and Fazal Rizvi. St. Leonards, Australia: Allen & Unwin. 54–68.

Robbins, Bruce. 2000. "Secularism, Elitism, Progress, and Other Transgressions: On Edward Said's 'Voyage In.' " *The Pre-Occupation of Postcolonial Studies.* Eds. Fawzia Afzal-Khan and Kalpana Seshadri-Crooks. Durham: Duke UP. 157–70.

Rockefeller, Steven C. 1992. "Comment." *Multiculturalism and "The Politics of Recognition": An Essay.* Charles Taylor. Ed. Amy Gutmann. Princeton: Princeton UP. 87–98.

Rothenberg, Jerome. 1988. "American Indian Poetry and 'Other' Traditions." *American Literature.* Ed. Boris Ford. Vol. 9 of *The New Pelican Guide to English Literature.* London: Penguin. 583–94.

Rothstein, Edward. 2001. "Attacks on U.S. Challenge the Perspectives of Postmodern True Believers." *New York Times,* 22 Sep.

———. 2005. "The Scholar Who Irked the Hindu Puritans." *New York Times,* 31 Jan.

Roy, Arundhati. 2003. *War Talk.* Cambridge: South End P.

Rushdie, Salman. 1991a. "Imaginary Homelands." *Imaginary Homelands: Essays and Criticism, 1981–1991.* London: Granta Books. 9–21.

———. 1991b. "The Location of Brazil." *Imaginary Homelands: Essays and Criticism, 1981–1991.* London: Granta Books. 118–28.

Safire, William. 2004. "On Language: The New Black." *New York Times,* Magazine Desk, 30 May.

Said, Edward W. 1978. *Orientalism.* New York: Pantheon Books.

———. 1983. "Traveling Theory." *The World, the Text, and the Critic.* Cambridge: Harvard UP. 226–47.

———. 1993. *Culture and Imperialism.* New York: Knopf.

———. 1994. *Representations of the Intellectual.* New York: Pantheon.

———. 1999. "An Unsolved Paradox." *MLA Newsletter* 117 (Summer): 3.

———. 2000. *Reflections on Exile and Other Essays.* Cambridge: Harvard UP.

———. 2001a. "Terror in America." *The Observer,* 16 Sep.: 27.

———. 2001b. "The Public Role of Writers and Intellectuals." *The Nation* 273.8: 27–33.

Salamon, Julie. 2004. "Online Magazine Removes Cultural Blinders." *New York Times,* 18 Feb.

Sanjek, Roger. 1993. "Anthropology's Hidden Colonialism: Assistants and Their Ethnographers." *Anthropology Today* 9.2 (Apr.): 13–18.

San Juan, Jr. E(pifanio). 1991. "The Cult of Ethnicity and the Fetish of Pluralism: A Counter Hegemonic Critique." *Cultural Critique* 18 (Spring): 215–29.

———. 1992. *Racial Formations/Critical Transformations: Articulations of Power in Ethnic and Racial Studies in the United States.* Atlantic Highlands: Humanities P.

———. 1995. *Hegemony and Strategies of Transgression: Essays in Cultural Studies and Comparative Literature.* Albany: State U New York P.

———. 1998. *Beyond Postcolonial Theory.* New York: St. Martin's P.

————. 2002. *Racism and Cultural Studies: Critiques of Multiculturalist Ideology and the Politics of Difference.* Durham: Duke UP.

Saussure, Ferdinand de. 1965. *Cours de linguistique générale.* Paris: Payot.

Schaub, Diana. 2002. "The Pillars of the Temple of Liberty." *New Criterion* 20.8 (Apr.): 4–15.

Schor, Naomi. 1994. "Collecting Paris." *The Cultures of Collecting.* Eds. John Elsner and Roger Cardinal. Cambridge: Harvard UP. 252–74.

Schwab, Raymond. 1950. *La Renaissance orientale.* Paris: Payot.

————. 1984. *Oriental Renaissance: Europe's Rediscovery of India and the East, 1680–1880.* Trans. Gene Patterson-Black and Victor Reinking. Intro. Edward W. Said. New York: Columbia UP.

Scott, Joan Wallach. 1992. "Multiculturalism and the Politics of Identity." *October* 61 (Summer): 12–19.

————. 2002. "Higher Education and Middle Eastern Studies Following September 11, 2001." *Academe* 88.6: 50–55.

Sebastian, Sunny. 2001. "Rajasthan's 'Original Backwards' Rally for Justice." *The Hindu,* 28 May. http://www.hinduonnet.com/thehindu/2001/05/28/stories/142822b.htm.

Segalen, Victor. 1995. *Œuvres complètes.* Paris: R. Laffont.

Sengupta, Somini. 2007. "Indian Officials to Rule How 'Backward' Group Is." *New York Times,* 5 Jun.

Shohat, Ella. 1992. "Notes on the Post-Colonial." *Social Text* 31–32: 99–113. Also appears in *The Pre-Occupation of Postcolonial Studies.* Eds. Fawzia Afzal-Khan and Kalpana Seshadri-Crooks. Durham: Duke UP. 126–39.

————. 1995. "The Struggle over Representation: Casting, Coalitions, and the Politics of Identification." *Late Imperial Culture.* Eds. Román de la Campa, E. Ann Kaplan, and Michael Sprinker. London: Verso. 166–78.

————, and Robert Stam, eds. 2003. *Multiculturalism, Postcoloniality, and Transnational Media.* New Brunswick: Rutgers UP.

Slemon, Stephen. 1992–93. "Teaching at the End of Empire." *College Literature* 19–20.3–1: 152–61.

————. 1995. "Introductory Notes: Postcolonialism and Its Discontents." *Ariel* 26.1 (Jan.): 7–11.

Sokal, Alan. 1996a. "A Physicist's Experiments with Cultural Studies." *Lingua Franca* (May–Jun.): 62–64.

————. 1996b. "Transgressing the Boundaries: Toward a Transformative Hermeneutics of Quantum Gravity." *Social Text* 46–47 (Spring–Summer): 217–52.

————, and Jean Bricmont. 1997. *Impostures intellectuelles.* Paris: O. Jacob.

————. 1998. *Fashionable Nonsense: Postmodern Intellectuals' Abuse of Science.* New York: Picador.

Solzhenitsyn, Alexandr. 1974. *The Gulag Archipelago, 1918–1956: An Experiment in Literary Investigation.* Trans. Thomas P. Whitney. New York: Harper & Row.

Sowell, Thomas. 2004. *Affirmative Action around the World: An Empirical Study.* New Haven: Yale UP.

Spivak, Gayatri Chakravorty. 1985. "The Rani of Sirmur: An Essay in Reading the Arcives." *History and Theory* 24.3: 247–72.

———. 1986. "Imperialism and Sexual Difference." *Oxford Literary Review* 8.1–2: 225–40.

———. 1988a. "Can the Subaltern Speak?" *Marxism and the Interpretation of Culture.* Eds. Cary Nelson and Lawrence Grossberg. Urbana: U Illinois P. 271–313.

———. 1988b. *In Other Worlds: Essays in Cultural Politics.* London: Routledge.

———. 1991. "The Making of America's New Literary History, the Teaching of English, and the Future of Cultural Studies." *New Literary History* 21.4: 781–98.

———. 1993. *Outside in the Teaching Machine.* New York: Routledge.

———. 1995. "Ghostwriting." *Diacritics* 25.2 (Summer): 64–84.

———. 1999. *A Critique of Postcolonial Reason: Toward a History of the Vanishing Present.* Cambridge: Harvard UP.

———. 2003. *Death of a Discipline.* New York: Columbia UP.

Srikanth, Rajini. n.d. "The World is Only a Mouse-Click Away: Internet Readers, Translated Texts, and the Collecting of Cultures." Unpublished manuscript.

Srinivas, Mysore Narasimhachar. 1952. *Religion and Society among the Coorgs of South India.* Oxford: Clarendon P.

———. 1956. "A Note on Sanskritization and Westernization." *Far Eastern Quarterly* 15.4: 481–96.

———. 1966. *Social Change in Modern India.* Berkeley: U California P.

Srivastava, Aruna. 1995. "Postcolonialism and Its Discontents." *Ariel* 26.1 (Jan.): 12–17.

Stevens, Wallace. 1972. *The Palm at the End of the Mind: Selected Poems and a Play.* Ed. Holly Stevens. New York: Vintage Books.

Stewart, Susan. 1993. *On Longing: Narratives of the Miniature, the Gigantic, the Souvenir, the Collection.* Durham: Duke UP.

Suleri, Sara. 1992. *The Rhetoric of English India.* Chicago: U Chicago P.

Sunder Rajan, Rajeswari. 1997. "The Third World Academic in Other Places; or, the Postcolonial Intellectual Revisited." *Critical Inquiry* 23.3 (Spring): 596–616.

Talbot, Margaret. 2001. "Other Woes." *New York Times,* Magazine Desk, 18 Nov.

Taylor, Charles. 1992. *Multiculturalism and "The Politics of Recognition": An Essay.* Ed. Amy Gutmann. Princeton: Princeton UP.

———. 1994. *Multiculturalism: Examining the Politics of Recognition.* Ed. Amy Gutmann. Princeton: Princeton UP.

Thernstrom, Stephen, and Abigail Thernstrom. 1997. *America in Black and White.* New York: Simon and Schuster.

Thomas, R. Roosevelt. 1990. "From Affirmative Action to Affirming Diversity." *Harvard Business Review* 69 (Mar.–Apr.): 107–17.

Todorov, Tzvetan. 1982. *La conquête de l'Amérique: La question de l'autre.* Paris: Seuil.

———. 1984. *The Conquest of America: The Question of the Other.* Trans. Richard Howard. New York: Harper & Row.

Veyne, Paul. 1971. *Comment on écrit l'histoire: Essai d'épistémologie.* Paris: Seuil.

Wald, Alan. 1991. *The Campaign against "Political Correctness": Analysis of a Frame-up and Proposals for a Socialist Response. A Solidarity Discussion Paper.* Pamphlet. Detroit: Solidarity.

Waters, Anne B. 1997. "The Predicaments of Women: The Family and the State in the Construction of Subjectivity in Maharashtra, India." PhD diss., University of Michigan.

White, Kenneth. 1987. *L'esprit nomade.* Paris: B. Grasset.

Wolff, Janet. 1993. "On the Road Again: Metaphors of Travel in Cultural Criticism." *Cultural Studies* 7.2: 224–39.

Zantop, Susanne. 1997. *Colonial Fantasies: Conquest, Family, and Nation in Precolonial Germany, 1770–1870.* Durham: Duke UP.

Žižek, Slavoj. 1997. "Multiculturalism or the Cultural Logic of Multinational Capitalism." *New Left Review* 225 (Sep.–Oct.): 28–51.

———. 2002. *Welcome to the Desert of the Real! Five Essays on September 11 and Related Dates.* London and New York: Verso.

Index